Granny Nancy

IRELAND'S OLDEST LADY

Who Lived, Loved and Laughed For 107 Years

A magical and inspiring story captured by her granddaughter Louise Coghlan. As the world stood still in a pandemic, Granny Nancy stood forward!

LOUISE COGHLAN

First Published In Ireland In 2022

Some details within this text have been changed to respect the privacy of individuals.

ISBN: 978-1-3999-3674-3

Cover design: Rebecacovers

Printed and bound in Ireland by
printmybook.com
a subsidiary of
Carraig Print Litho Press Limited,
Ballinbrittig, Carrigtwohill, Co. Cork.

All photographs were taken by Louise Coghlan apart from those identified within from Elaine McCrossan and Seamus Farrelly.

PRAISE FOR GRANNY NANCY & LOUISE COGHLAN

Sahm Venter - Journalist and Editor of 'The Prison Letters of Nelson Mandela'

" It struck me on my first meeting with Louise, shortly after Granny Nancy's death, that she was a storyteller bursting with detail about their antics as well as anecdotes about her grandmother's wisdom and nurturing nature.

Louise has written a book we can all relate to, that generations to come will benefit from. The tale of a grandmother and granddaughter navigating an international emergency and how they invited us all in, to live and love and learn with them. "

Anne Marie Kelly - Broadcaster and Award Winning Documentary Maker

" So I met Granny Nancy when she turned 100 and instantly, I fell in love with her. Her home, the nooks and crannies, the tea, the fire, the glow, particularly the glow of her lovely face. "

Ciaran Mullooly - Former RTE Midlands Correspondent

" I recorded an interview with Nancy that day for RTE Television and radio and it got one of the largest responses I ever received over a career lasting well beyond 25 years in broadcasting. Looking into the camera, with a wicked sense of urgency in her voice, Nancy said the Minister for Housing needed to provide homes at an affordable rate for the many people around the country who have no home of their own and were staying in hotels and other accommodation. "

Luan Parle - Irish Musician and Songwriter

"In April 2020, when everybody was isolating at home with their loved ones due to COVID and the restrictions imposed, I called Louise and Granny Nancy to ask them if they would help me out and take part in a video for a single I was releasing. I was delighted when they agreed. They sent me the most marvellous footage of them both dancing and bopping about at home to the song, which really captured the incredible spirit, fun, and love for life that Granny Nancy possessed."

Cliona O'Hagan - Irish Country Music Singer

"I asked Lou if her Gran told her the secret of life and instantly she said Cliona you already said it! I said "did I?" And I asked what was it that I said? She said her Granny said "balance" was the secret of life. Work to live, not live to work! I was just mesmerised by this."

Fr. Bryan Shortall - Irish Author and National Director for the Padre Pio Apostolate

"I was privileged to have a chat with Granny Nancy on the phone and it was wonderful to speak to her and hear how real the good Lord was to her and how readily she would "thank God and his blessed mother and all the saints" I remain grateful to God for meeting Louise and being introduced to a mighty woman who lived through many generations."

Mike McBride - BBC Northern Ireland Journalist

"Granny Nancy and Louise were both incredibly chatty and many times when I was speaking with them, I felt like I was the one being interviewed. They were incredibly warm, friendly, and funny - Granny Nancy had a particularly wicked sense of humour and an incredibly infectious laugh."

Mairead Ronan - TV Presenter and Broadcaster

"Of all the interviews I've done on radio over the years, my chat with Nancy has stayed with me to this day. Her positivity, kindness and message of hope genuinely touched so many of the listeners too."

Wallis Bird - Irish Award Winning Musician

"Two good eggs nested together, forever and always"

Fr. Richard Gibbons, Parish Priest and Rector of Knock Shrine

"The story of Granny Nancy touched the hearts of so many, myself included. She was a wonderful Christian with a very kind outlook on life and no doubt she will be remembered forever more as the lady who stood forward with a bright light as darkness fell on our country and our world."

Eddie Rowley - Showbiz Editor, Sunday World Newspaper

"Thanks to her devoted and loving granddaughter, Louise, Nancy kept pace with the rapid changes in her twilight years. She was able to make her mark by connecting with people in the modern age on social media platforms such as Facebook and YouTube until the end of her days."

Louise Walsh - Journalist and LMFM Producer

"We only saw glimpses into Nancy's and Louise's Covid-19 Clonard world but we had no doubt, we wanted to see more. To feel involved more and to laugh more. We wanted to say we were friends with Nancy and Louise. That world will now come to light through Louise's book about the times she shared with her adored gran. Nancy was Louise's world and Louise was Nancy's world. And we can now be a little bit of that world."

Granny Nancy was a flower to us all.

Granny Nancy

October 16th 1913 - September 10th 2021

Once an Angel on Earth
and
Now a Saint in Heaven!

WHO IS LOUISE COGHLAN?

Louise Coghlan is a writer, speaker and communicator from County Kildare, Ireland. She has donned many hats in her working life but her most recent undertaking was to cocoon with her 107 year old grandmother Granny Nancy which was her most rewarding. Her writing has been published in *The Irish Independent*, *U Magazine* and *The Irish Times*. She has also worked as a full time journalist for *The Offaly Topic* while also working for national radio station Newstalk as a researcher and contributing documentaries and being a guest panellist on Midlands 103. Louise also ran her own marketing company Ceol PR for many years helping artists and entertainers across the country. Whilst cocooning with Granny Nancy, Louise interviewed her grandmother many times and this book is very much a book of love and a faithful keeping of Louise's final promise to her best friend to bring it to fruition. This is Granny Nancy's story and Louise believes the final gift that Granny left were her words of wisdom and hope to help us all keep going when times are tough. As part of their time living together, Louise and Granny set up a Facebook Page called '*Living and Laughing with Lou*' and through their nightly chats, prayers, cups of tea, they build up quite the following which in turn they lovingly refer to as their "*Facebook Family*". From baking together, dressing up, laughing, smiling and sharing their optimistic outlook even in the darkest hours of the pandemic, Granny Nancy and Lou won the hearts of everyone who entered their Facebook home. Now standing at an impressive 20,000 Facebook Family members, Lou is still as active and loving as ever with those who began their journey with her. This book has lots of aspects of the magic of the Facebook Family within it but mostly it's Louise's love for her Granny and best friend that shines through.

All Lou's mischief, messing, hope, healing and humour can be located on her Facebook page: *www.facebook.com/livingandlaughingwithlou*

All extra details and information can be found on Lou's website: *www.livingandlaughingwithlou.com*

Lou also writes a very uplifting Substack Newsletter/produces a mini podcast every Monday and Friday which is gaining great traction by the day and can be found here: *www.livingandlaughingwithlou.substack.com.*

And Lou is also on Instagram, Tik Tok and Twitter too, come join her in any of these very social spaces! She would love to have you on her bus! #beepbeep

It was Louise's love of the sky that led to the phrase of "Keep Looking Up"

This book is dedicated to Granny Nancy x
With love in my heart for you always.
Thank you for all you taught me and for all the love, tea and chats we shared and I'll forever look up to you x

This book is also dedicated to my wonderful mam Olive, my dear family and much loved friends.
Mam is my inspiration in my effort to lead a good life and I would not be the person I am today without her by my side.
Thank you for your support and love each and every day,
Love you always and forever,
Louise x

I would also like to include a special mention here to my five youngest best friends - Anthony, Nathan, Lauren, Josh and Shauna Logan who fill my heart with happiness and forever make me smile x

Also I would like to take a moment to remember all the beautiful people who passed away during the pandemic and particularly in the lockdown periods where funerals, hugs and sincere human connection was lost.
I think of all who died at that time and a special mention to all the families left behind broken during that period. You will always be in my prayers and never forgotten x

THANK YOU

Before you turn the next page, I just want to say ***THANK YOU*** so much for buying this book. It means so much to me and I hope it brings you as much healing, hope and happiness as it did me putting it together. Granny Nancy was a very special beacon of light in this world and particularly as we met with Covid for the first time, she really rose to the occasion in so many ways. I know she would want me to ***THANK YOU*** for loving her as you did and for all the love and kindness you showed both myself and herself. Her 107th birthday was her best birthday ever [her words] and that was because of all the cards, love, presents, phone calls and messages you all sent and of course her unforgettable birthday drive by organised by her friends, neighbours, family and the local community of Clonard in County Meath.

May this book sit on your shelf for one hundred and seven years and ***may you have a lifetime of happiness and health to match.***

If ever there is a day your troubles are heavy, take this book into your hands and remember if Granny Nancy could do it, so can you. Look up to Heaven if you need her and just ask her to help, and I promise she will.

I will always be here for you in any way I can and be sure to know, no matter how dark the day gets or how heavy your heart feels, just remember to
'***Keep Looking Up!***'

Love and Light always,

Lou and Granny Nancy x

A selection and reminder of all the good times and memories made with Lou and Granny Nancy.

CONTENTS

Gran looking lovely and content at home in Clonard in County Meath.

FOREWORD

IN LOVING MEMORY OF NANCY STEWART

I first met Nancy in 2013 when she was a young and spritely 101 years of age! My first meeting with her, sadly, was at the wake of her son-in-law, Joe Coghlan, in Ballyonan House, Broadford. I remember that after I had said the rosary for Joe, I sat beside Nancy and we talked together about the sad mystery of suffering and death. In so far as I left the matter an open question, Nancy quickly gave me the perfect Christian answer. She told me the story of how her husband, Bob, was killed in a car accident in 1989 and how she was seriously injured in that car accident herself. That accident happened when they were turning into Clonard Church to go to Mass! And yet, with the unquestioning faith of a saint, Nancy told me that she accepted that tragedy as God's Holy Will and she also said that whenever we are faced with tragedies, we must trust in God and believe that He will make all things right in the end. From that moment on, I was in awe of Nancy and regarded her as a living saint, a person who was very close to God. So, that was my first impression of Nancy Stewart, and every time I met her afterwards only consolidated the fact that my first impression of her was absolutely correct.

Granny Nancy Stewart was propelled onto a world stage by her granddaughter, Louise Coghlan, who creatively used the Facebook social media platform, to introduce "*Granny Nancy*" to many millions of people worldwide. And I was one of those many people who were inspired by Nancy's wise words, simple faith and sincere prayer all throughout the time of the pandemic.

Sadly, Irish people today are a lot less religious than they were in the past. I wonder if that's a good thing? I wonder if Irish people are happier today than the people of Nancy's generation? I wonder if we would be better off without people like Nancy Stewart? Absolutely not! In fact, I know for sure that Ireland will be worse off without good people like Nancy Stewart. The fact of the matter is, we desperately need good people like Granny Nancy in modern Ireland. In my opinion, there is nothing we need more in our country at this moment in time than good mothers and good grandmothers! Because without Catholic influencers like Nancy Stewart, Ireland will inevitably lose its Celtic Soul, its Celtic Spirituality and its Christian Heritage.

In this wonderful book which has been written about the life of Nancy Stewart by her devoted granddaughter, Louise Coghlan, we can read all about the unique and inspiring life of Granny Nancy. We can also look at the many colourful photographs which Louise took of Granny Nancy and which capture many and various aspects of her life which are natural, funny, sad, spiritual, motherly, compassionate and saintly. Louise's book celebrates Granny Nancy's life with great gladness and thanksgiving. And that is absolutely the right thing to do one year after Nancy's death. Louise's book is much more emotional than rational, much more feelings than thoughts, much more heart stuff than head stuff. Her book was written from the heart and it invites all of us to lovingly remember Granny Nancy's heart of gold, a heart that was full of laughter and joy, full of faith, prayer and good works, full of God's grace and compassion.

Louise's personal tribute to her beloved granny was a labour of love. However, love hurts. It wasn't easy for Louise to write this book. A lot of grief came to the surface. A lot of loneliness was felt. A lot of tears were shed. But Louise kept on looking up and kept on writing; and because of her indomitable persistence and stamina, we are now privileged to be able to hold in our hands this very precious book about Granny Nancy and to read all about this extraordinary woman who was graced by God with a life that took her into her 108th year, a long and wonderful life that was very much cherished and adored by all members of her family and very much appreciated and respected by her many friends and neighbours and by her local parish community and by her huge Facebook family all across the world!

Congratulations to Louise for writing this very special book and for giving us this unique insight into Nancy's soul; a soul which is now enjoying the peace and happiness of heavenly glory.

Ar dheis Dé go raibh a anam.
Fr. Gerard Breen
Former Parish Priest of Balyna Parish, County Kildare.

PROLOGUE

WHO WAS GRANNY NANCY?

Granny Nancy [also known as Nancy Stewart] was a lady who lived on the planet for over one hundred and seven years and three hundred and twenty-eight days. Granny Nancy was not only the oldest lady in Ireland, but she was also the oldest lady living in her own home in 2021.

Nancy was my grandmother and my very best friend throughout the pandemic, and I feel it's important to share with you her spirit, her magic and her personality because not only do I know that nobody like Granny Nancy will ever walk this earth again but also I feel very strongly that in reading about the life of Granny Nancy you will feel the warmth, the hope, the resilience and love of her heart and in a moment where the world seems quite confused and chaotic, this cute little lady will help you to keep going.

On September 10th, 2021, around 5.45 am Granny Nancy let go of my hand and took hold of God's, when she left this earth to take up her new seat in Heaven. My heart instantly shattered but within the million pieces of my hurt for her departing, she left me with something much bigger than I could have ever imagined. She left me with her story.

For thirty-two months I lived alongside my dear beloved grandmother but for thirty-seven years I was blessed with her as my best friend. With the pandemic arriving without notice, I instantly and intensely took situ beside her at her Jubilee stove not knowing what was about to begin. For many, the pandemic was a curse, but it was only as the hours, days and months passed that I realised for me, it was far from a curse instead, it was a wonderful miraculous blessing. A chapter in my life where I got to study, embrace, love, laugh and breath in my darling grandmother from every angle, inch and heartbeat. We grew into each other as we cocooned night and day with only the essential family and carers stepping inside our world. I never knew how long this moment was going to last but I knew it was an incredibly special moment and I lived and loved every second of it with Granny.

I captured much of our shenanigans on my phone through videos, photos and most importantly in my heart. I knew I was after being blessed with the honour and the opportunity to care for and love my Granny in the last days of her life, but we lived them like we were only beginning. We reached out to the world through our social media page '*Living and Laughing with Lou*' and the world reached back. The world not only found Granny fascinating, but they fell in love with her and her with them and that's where the magic happened. And as we say here in Ireland, the rest is history.

I know I'm slightly biased, but I believe as the book develops, you will agree with me that she really was a real-life miracle and someone very special. As she shared her story, I realised she was no longer just my Granny, she became everyone's Granny. Me and Gran spoke of this book many times. I interviewed her lots as we cocooned, and we used to laugh saying will we ever get this book written? Gran would say to me the following;

"*You must have all my story now in that computer of yours! My life is not very interesting but I've loved every second of it. I've cried, I've had my heart broken many times but I'm still here smiling. If anything comes from this book only for someone somewhere to know that you can keep going no matter what happens to you, well then Louise we have done good.*"

So here it is. Our book. But very much Granny's book told through the simple format of questions and answers and lots of colour. Turn over this page and let the magic of Granny Nancy seep into your soul and bring a bright light into your day wherever you may be reading this. And thanks so much for buying our book. It means so much to me on earth and I know Gran is beaming with pride up in Heaven.
God bless you all and keep you safe.

And don't forget '***Keep Looking Up!***'

Lou x

BACKGROUND TO GRANNY NANCY

A photo I captured of Gran which just makes me smile.

Nancy was born on the 16th of October 1913. That was a long time ago, wasn't it? Even to try and imagine the world that Granny Nancy was born into is nearly unimaginable at this stage. Nancy was born before Ireland was free of English rule and lived through not only the world wars of her time but also the independence of the state along with a historical time when women were not allowed to vote or even have much say.

As I am typing this, Nancy is sitting in her warm cosy armchair by her Jubilee stove in the small village of Clonard in the county of Meath approximately thirty-five miles from Dublin city, with her three rosary beads around her left arm and sipping on a mug of tea. She recently turned one hundred and seven years young and has never been happier in life. I'm writing this story as she sits beside me and so we begin our chat with both of us very relaxed, cosy, drinking tea and very much at home in every way possible. We live together, we laugh together, and we love together so here begins the story of one hundred and seven year old Granny Nancy. We hope you enjoy x

Granny was very proud of our 'Nancy & Lou' Birthday Mugs gifted from Catriona Maguire marking Gran's 107th birthday.

CHAPTER ONE
GRANNY NANCY & GROWING UP

Granny Nancy is pictured here wearing a white dress and a bow in her hair to the left of the photo. She was the youngest of six children & is pictured with her sister Mag & Bess and brothers John, Mick & Jimmy Bird and her beautiful mam Margaret. This photo was taken in 1917.

Granny Nancy, let's talk about your childhood years. The day when God brought you into the world. You were born on October 16th, 1913. Your childhood must have been a fair bit different to mine as I only landed on the earth in 1983. Let's go back together in time to your earlier days with your family.

Who was in your family as a child?

There was six of us as children in the house. There was Elizabeth who we called Bess, Jimmy, John, Nancy [that's me], Mick and Mag. Six of us altogether. It was a lot, wasn't it compared to families nowadays when you think of it. Nobody would have six children really anymore. Funny how times have changed.

Did ye ever fall out with each other?

I'm sure we did! We often had rows among ourselves about auld footballs or whatever we would be playing but that would be it. Nothing serious that I can really remember because it was all only stuff all children quarrel about.

What were the sleeping arrangements like with so many children living together?

We had bedrooms for all the children. One room the girls were in, and the boys were in another and then our parents were in their own bedroom. We had a big bed and a small bed in the room. Many a time at night you would hear us children crossing over to each other's rooms to get in with each other. Lovely memories really. We got on really well as siblings.

Were ye good kids?

I think we were but I'm not sure. [As she giggles to herself].

Where was home for you as a child?

Castlerickard in County Meath was my home when I was growing up. My mam's name was Margaret Harnan and my dad was John Bird. Mam was originally from Rathmoylan in County Meath but moved to Castlerickard once she married my father. I had a good childhood. My mam was lovely and so was my father. My father was a blacksmith. He was a nice man. He shoed the horses and did loads of work for people. He was a quiet man. I never remember him being cross with us. He died very young which always saddened me as a child, but we got through it. When he died, my mam had to find a way to support us. My mam was a lovely quiet woman, she would only ever raise her voice if we were really acting the maggot as children. She was a strong woman and a great woman, and we were very lucky to have her as our mother.

What did your mam do when your dad passed?

When the post office came up for tender in the area, she applied for it and got it. It was a big deal and she had to do lots of training to start it up. I would have been ten or eleven when she got it. When mam was running the post office, we would be sent down to the haggard or put down the back of the house especially if someone important was coming in. It was a very busy post office. Back then it was a great service to be able to send someone a letter. There was no other way to communicate. And if anyone, got a telegram . . . well there would be some excitement. It was the bee's knees. I remember my mam getting one once from an aunt of hers and the excitement! It was so much more expensive to get a telegram but the special part was that you would receive it within three hours. A letter would take three days so only something important or on a special occasion would anyone receive a telegram.

Gran pictured outside her home in her younger years.

What time did you go to bed as a child?

Half six or seven in the wintertime. We would have to say the rosary before bed every night without fail. We wouldn't be let go to bed without saying the rosary. In the summertime, we would be let stay out playing until seven or eight o'clock. Then back inside to say our five decades of the rosary. We would take it in our turns every night. We were so used to it; we didn't actually mind. When you are used to something, you don't mind doing it, so saying the rosary was just part of our bedtime ritual and it didn't do us any harm! If anything, it was good for us. To this day I still say my rosary a good few times during the day and every night before I close my eyes as well. I wouldn't be able to sleep without it. It gives me great peace and great comfort. And I think it calms my mind It's a great way of ending the day with a peaceful habit and I always thank God then as well for all he has given me during the day.

Who else called to your house apart from people visiting the post office?
The breadman, a fishman, the milkman, a vegetable man and then of course someone would call with groceries if they were going to Trim. Back then lots of people would not only call for a visit and a chat but also all our needs were met by travelling work people whether delivering your milk, your bread, your groceries or whatever you might need.

If I was to say to you Granny, you had a good childhood would that be a true statement?
Yes, very much so Louise. I only remember good times thank God. We were never short of anything, and I got on with my siblings very well and my mam was wonderful. Sure what else would a child need after that. We had enough to eat, a roof over our head and back then you were very grateful for that alone. We also had great fun with all our friends and neighbours and thank God my childhood was a very happy time.

Your last immediate family member to pass was your sister Mag who you were very close to. That must have been very hard on you. I remember Aunt Mag well myself, she was such a kind lady, just like you Gran. Ye were very similar weren't ye?
Aw yes, I loved all my brothers and sisters, but I was especially close to Mag in the end because we were the two last standing. Mag was married to Hugh, and we were the best of friends the three of us. I guess in life we never know who is going to leave in what order, but I was very grateful to have had Mag for so long. She was a great sister, and we had the best of times. I loved all my brothers and my other sister Bess just as much, but it was just Mag was the last of the family to leave. Who was to know I was going to still be here one hundred and seven years later. I'll enjoy meeting them all again when my time comes, but not just yet.

Granny Nancy having fun and laughs with her sister Mag McGrath and Mag's husband Hugh.

Granny in her young days in one of her favourite seats in her home in Clonard.

Bob and Nancy looking very happy on their wedding anniversary in Clonard.

CHAPTER TWO
GRANNY NANCY AND FAMILY

Gran cherished this photo of herself, Bob and their six children
Back: Olive, Margaret (RIP), Anne (RIP), Kathleen, Mary
Front: Finian, Granny, Bob (RIP).

When did you get married Gran?
I got married around 23 or 24. I got married to Bob Stewart. I knew him a year or two. He was the only boyfriend I ever had.

Where did u meet him?
I met him on the road! That's the way it was back then. We used to be sitting under a big old tree down at Castlerickard where I was born and we just chatted and became good friends. And from that friendship, came our marriage and that was that!

How did he propose?
It was kind of funny when I think back. Bob said to me "do you think will

we get married Nancy?" and I replied without a second thought, "sure I think we will Bob!" They really were simple times, but I loved it!

What church did you get married in?

We got married in Ballivor because back then you always got married in the woman's parish. Fr. O'Farrell married us, and I remember us going home to Castlerickard after the ceremony. My wedding dress was a long dress with lace at the top. I cut it up afterwards and made it into a short frock. Back then Trim had lovely shops and we all loved going to Trim for our dresses. I think I bought it for ten pounds. It would be a terrible lot of money to pay back then but I got my value out of it and I loved it. Trim still has lovely shops, doesn't it?

Bob and his wife Nancy on their wedding day.

What did you do after the wedding?

We had our breakfast at home where the post office was. It was my mother's old home and my home as a child. We had a big breakfast of rashers and sausages. Sausages were such a big treat back then. Not like now. Then we went to Dublin for our honeymoon for two nights to the Gresham Hotel. Two nights in Dublin was our honeymoon and we loved it. We went out and walked the streets and it was really lovely. We came home on the bus to Clonard and walked up the village back home to Bob's house. Our family was minding the house and when we arrived back, they had a lovely big meal waiting for us. It was so nice, and we were so thrilled.

Granny and Bob celebrating their 50th Wedding Anniversary.

We're sitting in that house you and Bob walked up to now aren't we Granny? Gosh this is a very special house really. Did ye make changes to it?

After a while being married, we started to do a few little bits to the house to improve it. It was an old wall inside here. George Hickey built a lovely cement wall for us and we were thrilled. He put in new windows for us too when we had the money saved up. And he made that door frame there for us as well. God, he was a great man for jobs. So able and talented do you know what I mean? He could sort any problem and we were very grateful. I've got new windows since because you know nowadays these new windows are all the fashion. I have to say I love my windows. They are small old type windows but nowadays they are great to keep the cold out. We were lucky when Bob got us a range as well instead of the big open fire. It's the same range I have to this day, and it's never let me down. Sure back then the range was such a big deal. It did everything. You could cook on it, and it would keep us all warm as well.

Granny with Margaret and Anne and Anne's daughter Tara.

You had six children Granny. That was a big family.
Yes, I had six beautiful children. I had five girls and one boy. I had Kathleen, Finian, Margaret and Anne, Mary and Olive. Two of the girls were twins. They were quite a surprise I can tell you. I thought I was only having one child and then the midwife/nurse said hold on Nancy you're about to have a second child. I gave birth to all my children upstairs here in this house. I loved all my children. They were great when they were small. Now I'm not saying it wasn't hard work running a house with six children, but I enjoyed every second of it.

Sadly, I lost both the twins in recent years. Margaret got that terrible disease Motor Neurone. Sure it was so hard to watch her go downhill but she handled it so well. I was so sad to lose her. Then a few years later poor Anne passed too. Sure, she died of heartbreak without her sister. They were so close. Both got Kerry men over in England when they lived there and then both moved back to Tralee. I'm so lucky I still have the three girls living locally to me here. That's Kathleen, Olive and Mary. My son Finian lives in England but it's great, we get to talk on the phone every week.

Do you remember the car crash you were in with Bob?

I don't remember it when it happened. I don't remember going into the hospital or anything would you believe. I remember being in the hospital. I know a girl stayed with me when Bob's funeral was happening. That is a faint memory. But it was a tough moment in my life. We were going to mass that morning in Clonard. We pulled to the middle of the road and the car coming the other way was blinded by the sun and struck us. Bob went to Mullingar hospital, and I was very badly injured and was taken to Dublin. I was unconscious and I don't think I was given much hope to live would you believe? Poor Bob they thought was fine but unluckily he got a blood clot in his leg while in the hospital and didn't it travel to his heart and sadly, he passed away. He was buried by the time I came round. It was a huge shock to me and to the family to have to go through the funeral without me. It's not easy knowing your husband was buried and I wasn't even there. But one thing I knew was God was minding him from that day until this, and that gave me great strength. I never held anything against the other driver, we all make mistakes, and nobody was to be blamed.

Thank God I lived on and as you can see, I've done pretty well thank God. Those early years without Bob were not easy but I have a great family and they all minded me and were so good. I'll never forget what they did for me. And even now they are still minding me. Sure I couldn't be happier.

Family is very important to you Granny?

It is Louise. I've been very lucky to have a great family who love me, and I love them too. I've so many grandchildren, great-grandchildren and I even have great-great grandchildren. Would you believe that? Once everyone is well, that's all that matters to me. I think once you have your health you have everything.

Granny, your family has grown somewhat over the years, tell me a little about that?

Well now Louise, I'm so lucky with all my family. And thanks be to God, my family have been blessed with beautiful little children. There are too many to mention, I would be afraid I might forget some of them if I started naming them out. But I know I have a lot of grandchildren, great grandchildren and great great grandchildren! Ah it's great to see the generations grow and grow over the years and I love each and every one of them dearly.

Granny loved connecting with people, and here is an image of a special connection she had with one of her great-grandchildren Shauna age four.

A family photo taken at Granny and Bob's 50th Wedding Anniversary at home in Clonard

CHAPTER THREE
GRANNY NANCY & FOOD

Granny and myself did so much baking in the lockdowns and we had so much fun. I love these photos of her looking so happy.

Rumour has it Granny Nancy, that you love your food! I have seen you clear your plate once or twenty times! You really enjoy good food and I think it's part of why you are so healthy and so well.

Tell us about your relationship with food?
I love food. A certain amount to keep me well has brought me this far, so

I don't think it has done me any harm. If anything, it has given me such a long and healthy life. I truly believe good plain food is important for a healthy life. I eat the same kind of food every day and all at the same time.

Have you always been a good eater?

Always. I never went without a meal [as she laughs]. You just ate what you were given and never questioned it when you were young and I'm the same up to this very day. Plain food. Bread and butter. Rashers and puddings were popular back in the day and I still love them [laughs again]. Sausages were a pure luxury when I was a child. I don't remember much about them even being eaten as they were that rare in my time. If you heard someone saying they had sausages, they were very fancy altogether. Mammy always had a plain normal dinner ready for us when we came home from school. Cabbage was a popular one on the plate.

As I myself was raising my own kids, we had our own little farm, and we would have killed a couple of pigs during the year. We would have one for the mill when the men came to do the thrashing and one at Christmas and that would do us for the year. You would put all the meat in straw and salt beside the fire that we had then. Of course, nowadays they want to get rid of our open fires. Have you ever heard such a malarkey. What are all these so-called smart people thinking? I hope we don't end up down the road with all these fancy houses not working so well and then they will regret forcing people to not have open fires. Anyways we would always dry out the pig beside the open fire. I know that doesn't sound nice, but it was the way at the time, and you would be very grateful for any food especially meat because it was a great way to keep the kids full and healthy. You would wrap the parts of pig up and store them in the shed. Simple as that and use the meat sparingly throughout the year and of course spread it around to neighbours and friends as well. We always shared back then. Nobody would ever keep everything for themselves. It was a time of sharing what you had because nobody really had much. But we always shared. Sharing with your neighbours and friends was a normal part of life and we were all grateful for this kindness between folk. We knew we were all in the same boat and nobody was really different. We all gave to each other and never thought twice about keeping extra for ourselves. The key was to make sure everyone around had enough for their families and then all the road would be happy together.

Granny enjoying her dinner as sits beside her cosy jubilee stove.

What did a Sunday mean to you when you had your own family to raise?
Sunday was the treat day of the week. It would be a six o'clock rise for me as a mother. I would come down and get the table ready. Then we would get the children all up. Next up was to light the open fire. My husband would head down the yard then. He would be milking the cows. We would have about fifteen or sixteen cows back then which was a lot of work. We only had two cows at the start and built up the numbers through a lot of grafting. I'd get the breakfast sorted while Bob was working down the yard. We would often put on a fry for a Sunday morning treat. Rashers and pudding with a big long toasting fork. We would have our breakfast here at the table in front of the fire with us all sitting down together. Loose tea was the only tea we had back then. Me and Bob would have the tea and there would be a sup of milk for the childer. The childer would then be sent upstairs to get dressed for mass.

We always went to Edenderry every Saturday ahead of our Sunday dinner and we would pick up fresh meat. We would pick up a bit of beef in the butcher as well. Ten or twelve shillings worth. I would sparingly share it out among us for our Sunday dinner after mass and then get

Monday's dinner out of it too. That's the way we did it back then. There was never any waste as we knew how hard it was to come across money and of course even meat was a treat.

Were there many different types of vegetables back then?

There wasn't many vegetables at that time. Cabbage and greens and turnips were all we really had. There wasn't carrots or parsnips. We didn't get them until later on in life. There wasn't much choice really so very different to the vegetable aisle nowadays in the shop. There was no such thing as I won't eat this, or I won't eat that. You would be left with nothing if you didn't eat what you had. You would never shove it back and get something different for your dinner if you didn't like what was on offer. Nowadays if there's three or four kids, they are all having different meals. It's a different world but I accept it for the modern times we are in as I love having the choice myself. It's a great country we live in that we have so much choice when it comes to food. Great farmers out there doing great work. I always hold a lot of respect and appreciation for the farmers in our country. Even with modern machines, farming is still a very hard job. It never ends and it can be very isolating on a farm working all year round with little breaks or support. It's really the only vocation left nowadays in this country, well alongside our few priests and nuns but after that, life choices are exactly that, choice driven, not for the love of a tradition. It's not a bad thing but it's admirable when someone chooses a job for the love of it. Farming is something you must love because as we all know it's an outdoor job and with the weather in Ireland, you would have to love your farming job to be out in all the weathers we get nowadays. Even if you have machines with farming, it's still seven days a week and when it's raining, you still have to go out to your field and you will still get wet in the rain. Some things will never change and that's not all bad.

You really love your food Granny. Why do you think that is?

Food is one of the reasons why I'm so good. I would never miss a meal. I love three good meals in the day and little snacks in between. Especially if someone comes in during the day we would always have a cup of tea and a biscuit of course. You can't be drinking a cup of tea with a friend and not have a biscuit!. I'm a fan of the plain rich tea ones myself but I love anything that appears with my cuppa. My granddaughter Grainne brings me buns on a Saturday, and I love them. But as for anyone who knows me, I never refuse any type of goodie with my cup of tea. Food is something I love, and it's kept me this well so I always say if you eat well, good plain food, you will live as long as me.

One thing I do about my meals is I like to keep my meals at the same time every day. I've always been like that as long as I can remember, and I tend to eat the same type of meals too. In the mornings, I usually have a cup of tea with my granddaughter Louise [that's you as she laughs to herself] around seven or half seven. We might watch mass and say a few prayers as well then. I love my first cup of tea when I wake. There is nothing like it out of a china mug. It's like the best thing in my life. I just love tea and that first cup starts my day off just so lovely in my bed. I couldn't be happier. We usually say an Our Father, a Hail Mary or two and then we always finish up with the Hail Holy Queen. Me and you both love that prayer don't we Louise?

We loved our 107th birthday mugs.

We sure do Granny. We do a lot of praying around food times that's for sure . . . it hasn't failed us yet.

I sometimes forget little bits of it, but you always bring me right back on track Louise. Sure prayers and a cup of tea to start my morning no wonder I'm so happy and I've got to live so long. Then I have my breakfast. One of my lovely carers then comes in with that. Sure I'm so lucky with all the people who are around me minding me and looking after me. I love my carers. They give Louise and my daughters a break and also they are my best friends. They have all been with me for years and they are family to me.

For my breakfast I always have Weetabix and then another big mug of tea and toast. I used to eat porridge years ago but I'm on the Weetabix now and I love it. I never leave a bit in the bowl as the girls will tell you. I'm a great woman for the grub. Then I have my little chat with the girls and get changed out of my pyjamas and into my day clothes. In the last year or so I haven't been getting out of bed till lunch time as with that old virus I have lost all my visitors. My family thank God have been so good to me and they visit me all the time but my home is not like it was before that Covid came in, so now I stay in bed until my lunch. I'm dressed but just not out in the kitchen.

My lunch is usually around half twelve. My daughter Mary cooks me carrots fresh in a pot and I love them in my hand here in the bed, just a few before my dinner. A little bit of salt and they are delicious. A bit like having a starter. Gosh I am a divil for the food, aren't I? [Laughing again]. Kathleen brings me up all lovely green cabbage and Olive brings me up dinners as well. Sure I couldn't be luckier or happier. The girls are great to me & I'd be lost without them. I'm so lucky they all live so close to me. In my younger days, and that was only a few years ago now [laughing again] I would have cooked all my own dinners and I loved it. I loved the smell in the back kitchen of potatoes, veg and a lovely piece of meat. Again I'm so lucky the girls mind me and take care of all the cooking for me. I usually have a lovely plain Irish dinner every day, it's what has kept me so well, I think. I love my potatoes and my vegetables and it's good to eat a bit of meat too. I love a bit of gravy or white sauce on top and then I'm very happy.

When I think back, I know where my love of white sauce comes from. My mother used to make white sauce for us as childer. It was a mix of flour and milk back then, not as easy as now to make it. But I loved it back then too. She would blend the flour and boil up the milk. It's much easier now making white sauce and sure it's great. So handy and no real tidying up either and it's just in the press with all the other goodies. When I clear my plate for dinner, I have my dessert then.

I never go without a dessert. Sure you're not living if you can't have a little treat for yourself. I'd eat anything to be honest. I'd always have a cup of tea with my dessert or maybe have it a little while after my dinner. There is nothing like a hot cup of tea around three o'clock.

Granny's favourite items, her rosary beads and her cup of tea.

Then you Louise would help take me out to my big black armchair by the stove after I've had my lunch and I'd love that. I'd be so happy to be out once I get out. You know that's often the case isn't it in life? Sometimes you think you couldn't be bothered and then when you do, you're happy you did if that makes sense. We'd have our tea together and a biscuit or two of course and have the chats. Later in the evening it would be time for more food.

My daughter Olive has given me my teatime meal for as long as I can remember. She never has missed an evening as long as my memory allows me to think back. I don't think I'd enjoy my tea without her if I'm honest. She's part of my teatime tradition and I'm always so delighted to see her come in the door because then I know it's tea time and I'm always so glad to see her as well.

Some days can be slow. It's something I've noticed as I got older. When you're not as able to move around freely or as independently the day can be long but I'm very lucky to have such good family and friends minding me. Mary and Kathleen, my two daughters are always in visiting me and doing jobs for me and Finian my son I get to chat to him on the phone because he lives in England. My granddaughter Ramona also rings me every morning without fail as well and I love to hear from her and my little great-grandchild Alannah. Thank God for the phone, it's great how technology has moved on really.

For my tea I could have anything these days. For as many years as I can remember, my stable evening meal every day was always a fry. Sausages, mushrooms, pudding, fried onions and fried bread and a cup of tea.

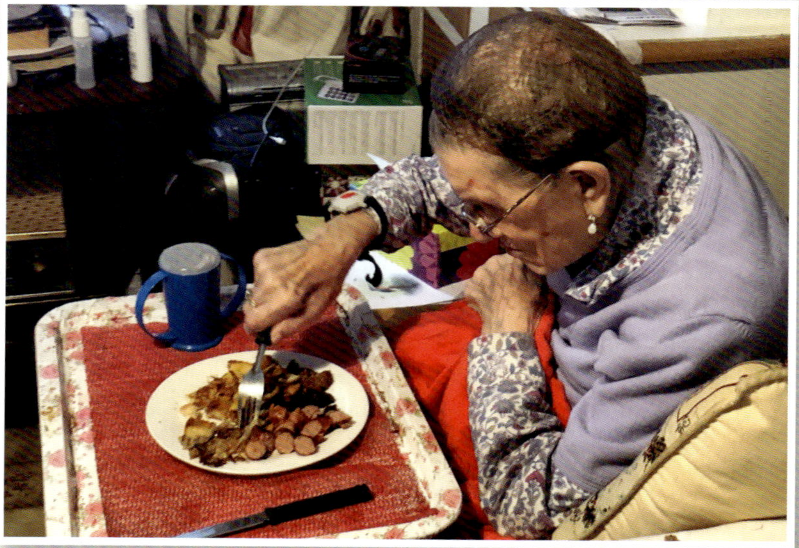

Granny loved her fry every day.

Oh I love the fried onions. We weren't too fond of eggs when I was a child and we always ended up having fried onions which I loved and still do to this day. My mam used to give us fried onions and potatoes. She'd chop up the onions and put them on the pan. You would have a big pot of potatoes and then you would mix them all up together. In those days, we didn't have much and when you got fed, you ate all you were given. You would be hungry because there was no such thing as snacks or food in between meals not like I love now [as she laughs]. When dinner or food was served you were starving, and nobody left anything behind.

We would be whipping one from the other, robbing from one another when my mother's head was turned. You wouldn't get that so much anymore because food is very much plentiful. It's good in one way but sometimes I think we are probably forgetful of how lucky we are to live in a time where there is so much food.

And then I think of the poor hungry childer in Africa and even many in our country who are homeless. We are lucky to live in a time where the shops are full of food but it's so important not to forget those less off. Not everyone is as lucky as me. That's why I always try to be grateful for what I have and also try to give money for the poor hungry childer. We should always try and share with others.

I've heard you love your egg in a mug, your guggie, these days Granny?
You're right Louise. Sure you know me; I love my egg in the mug now. If I'm not having a fry in the evenings, I love a guggie in a mug. It's something we've had all our lives in this house. It's a boiled egg, you take off the shell when it's cooked. I love a hard-boiled egg. I really wouldn't eat it any other way. So you take off the shell and then put it in a mug and then mash it up. Olive would do that for me and then pop in a little bit of butter and the most important part salt and pepper. Delicious along with a lovely slice of brown bread and butter and of course my favourite, my cup of tea. I love that. I usually have another little dessert or treat then after my tea. I might have a little bit of custard or maybe even a rich tea biscuit. Oh and not forgetting I love a jelly sweet before bed as well. You know the jelly babies are my favourite these days, those big juicy jellies. Athlone Sweets they are called, I think. Some evenings I'd say to Olive sure will I have one and sure she would always say, "Of course you will mam. Sure you were a good girl today and you will not

only have one, but two." Sure we would laugh together and I'd really enjoy it. I really do love my food. It must be what has kept me so well. Good plain food. Nothing fancy. God gave me a great appetite and he also gave me great health to be able to enjoy it all. I attribute my good long life to good eating.

Granny loved her guggie in a mug every day.

What's your favourite meal?

My favourite dinner would be a nice bit of bacon with turnips, cabbage and potatoes. Sure I love that. I also love lamb. I wouldn't do without potatoes. Once you have potatoes, you won't go hungry. We had our own potatoes out the back, our own crop back in the day. People always thought if you had them in the garden, they were nicer. I think they were right I guess, thinking back, but thank God potatoes nowadays are lovely too. And you don't even have to wash them. It's a great time to be alive really.

What's your favourite vegetable?

My favourite vegetables would be carrots, broccoli and cauliflower. I like the white sauce with the cauliflower if I'm having those. I love sauce I do. I like a lot of things, don't I? [As she laughs]

Granny loved her food and always said it played a huge part in her health and long life. Olive is in the background filling the fridge. Granny believed in having a fridgeful of food.

What is your favourite dessert?

My favourite dessert is rice pudding, but I do love strawberries and ice cream in the summer as well. I also love custard and jelly and if I'm honest there is nothing I would really refuse but my favourite dessert would be creamed rice pudding.

What is your favourite drink or is that a silly question Granny?

Oh Louise you know it because you love it too. We must be keeping Barry's in business these days the way me and you drink it together. My favourite drink is of course tea. And it must be Barry's. I love to keep my stomach full. I drink a lot of tea but I just love it. I wouldn't live without tea. Even when the kids were going to school, I'd get up earlier to have my cup of tea.

Granny loved our ice-cream evening we shared with the Facebook family every week.

Tea solves everything is my thinking. Before this old virus got a hold of us all, the kettle would never be off the boil in this house. I miss that. All my grandchildren would be coming in that door there in a line. And not forgetting my wonderful friends and my neighbours. I've been very lucky with the friends I have and all the lovely neighbours on this road. I'd never be stuck for anything. I don't know how I was so lucky to have so many good people in my life, and not forgetting my beautiful carers as well. I hope they all know how special they are to me. If they're reading this, I hope they know how grateful I am for them minding me so well and being my friend. I miss not having everyone here but please God we will be out of this soon and then we can all be back together. I look forward to that day and I know God won't let me down. We will get through this. We just need to be patient.

Speaking of tea granny, you remember the rationing of the tea way back in the day. Can you tell me about those days when the war was on?
The rationing of tea was a very hard time. As a household you would only get so much of it. If a family didn't like tea, we would give them some butter and they would give us their tea. I use to churn back then. So I'd give them butter and maybe some buttermilk as well. We always helped each out as neighbours. Thank God there is no such thing as rationing of tea nowadays, I don't think I could go through that again. I drink water as well but I'm not too fond of it so I put a drop of orange squash into it and then it's not too bad. It's important to drink water just to keep the body good. I like a sup of lemonade too. And even though it's an old idea, there is nothing better than boiled lemonade or 7up if you aren't feeling well. It hasn't let me down in all my years so if ever you aren't feeling great, boil the lemonade and all will be well again. I always have a bottle or two in the house, just in case.

What is your favourite jam?
Blackcurrant jam would be my favourite. To be honest I'd eat all of them and any of them. My favourites would include blackberry, gooseberry and rhubarb. I used to make them all in my younger days. They were hard work to make but so tasty. I'd have none left for myself after I'd make them because I'd have given them all away to callers and neighbours. When people came to the house all through my life, I'd always like to give them something and once I had jam in the press, I knew it was a nice little treat for anyone. It costs nothing to be nice and when someone is good to you, it's my pleasure to be good to them in return.

Do you like eating at the same time every day Granny?
Yes, I like to have my meals around the same time each day. I do think to myself sitting here, I wonder, is that what has helped keep me so good. I eat the same food each day around the same times. I wouldn't be cross if times got changed but my belly would notice. Oh and I always have my dinner at dinner time. It's an old fashion thing I guess people would say nowadays but it's done me no harm [as she laughs and rubs her belly].

Granny loved having a house full of food - She was gifted this for her 107th birthday and wasn't she thrilled!

CHAPTER FOUR

GRANNY NANCY AND FAITH

This is Granny watching mass virtually during the Covid 19 Lockdowns. She loved watching and listening to mass any way she could and embraced technology when the churches were physically closed for months on end.

How did ye travel to mass when you had your own family?

The children would go walking down the road themselves. They would collect children from along the road as they passed those houses, and all the children would walk to mass together. We followed down in the car after them. The children would have to wait for catechism after mass. The teacher sometimes would go through it with them and then the priest would examine the kids after that. It wasn't easy but it was worth it. They always learned something from it. And not to forget we got rid of them for the hour or two [as Nancy laughs]. It kept them out of trouble and it gave me a little break, there isn't a parent that wouldn't agree to that!! [Laughing again].

Would there be many people in mass?

Oh, it was always a big crowd at mass. The church would be full. The children would nearly always sit in the front seats. We all had our seats in which we sat too. Nobody would just go in and sit anywhere like we do nowadays. Bob and I had our seat in the short aisle and all the same people would sit in their seats. Everyone would be immaculately dressed. It was a lovely tradition really and you always felt good after it. And of course you would get to see all your neighbours and friends. I loved that part of it myself.

What happened after mass?

It would probably be half twelve when the kids returned home to us. They would head out to play out the back of the house. They would entertain themselves, maybe make babbie houses or play with an auld football.

Of course, before I'd let them go outside, I'd have to take off their good clothes and put them up for the next week. You would only have one set of good clothes back then and you would have to mind them. Not like nowadays where I think people have good clothes on every day. Back then your good clothes were so special. You knew you only had one set and really had to mind them like your life depended on them.

Your faith is very important to you Granny?

What? Is it? My face? Oh sorry I thought you were asking me is my face very important! [laughs to herself]. Oh my face is very important [laughs more]. They say it looks very young looking . . . what do you think Louise?

I think your face is the prettiest in the land Granny. Is your faith important to you Gran?

Oh it is yes. It is very important to me yes. When you have a good faith, it helps you get through hard things in life. It also helps you get through life. If you don't worry too much and depend on your faith, then you can get over any obstacle you meet. Life is full of troubles and problems, but I try not to think about them too much. Instead, I say a little prayer and ask God to help me. Also there is always someone worse off and then your worries seem small.

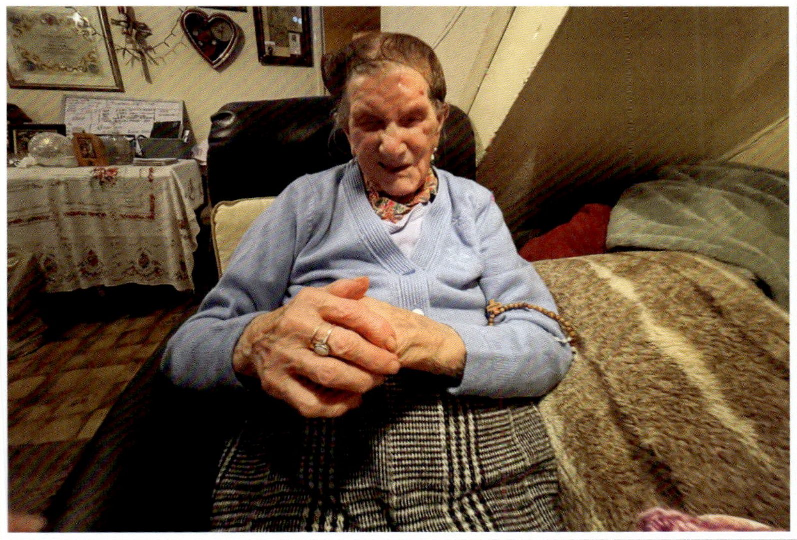

Myself and Granny had so many laughs . . . I loved capturing them on camera as there is nothing as joyful as seeing someone laugh.

What does the word faith mean to you Granny?

Well, what I'd call faith is to believe in God. And to ask him and the Blessed Virgin for things you would want or need. And in time you will get them. If it's only to bring back good faith to young childer or something small like that. No matter what you ask for, I believe in time you will receive it. Sometimes you have to be really patient but in time things always work out. My faith and my prayers have helped me through many hard times and God has never let me down.

With this virus here now, I pray every day to be safe through this pandemic and to keep all my family and friends safe and also I like to pray for anyone who has nobody to pray for them. Even if you think nobody is thinking of you, I promise I am.

If you haven't a prayer, I think you'll be slowed down in life. It helps to have a prayer. And I wouldn't miss mass on a Sunday either. I always brought my own childer to mass because I believe in God. And it's great now with the phone and the internet I can watch mass twenty times a day if I want. Louise, you're great with the phone. I hope it's not costing you a fortune, but I love when we watch mass together. Sure I've been across the country fifty times this week and it's really brilliant because I haven't left my armchair.

Do you believe there's a Heaven?

I do believe in heaven, but I'd love to see what it's like before I get there. They say hell is done away with now thank God. Some people who would be getting hard times, and disappointments, they might say hell is here on earth and I couldn't disagree with that. I just pray for everyone to be well and anyone who isn't well, I ask God to bring them back to good health if he can. If anyone can, God will. It's not easy to get through life if you're very sick. Or if you're sitting and can't get up. I'd say you would feel very bad in yourself. I feel so well I don't know what it's like to be sick thank God. I never remember being sick either which is a blessing.

I've been very lucky with my health. If someone is worried or if they have someone sick, I'd tell them to say prayers and ask God and his Blessed Mother to give them some relief that they could carry on and also I'd pray for them too. But I know it's so hard when the cross is heavy in life. We just have to keep going. Some people get it very hard and they don't be bad people at all. The very best of people get the hardest blows often. Well we don't know what's before us. We know what's behind us. And we must try to keep going as best we can day by day.

I loved watching the sun rising and setting outside Gran's home.

What does God mean to you?

God means everything to me. I ask himself and the Blessed Virgin and St. Joseph to keep us all safe. I have great faith in Padre Pio and St. Anthony for anything I need as well. I always ask them to help others. I have great faith in them all. I promise them money for the poor hungry childer. I promise to give them money and I do every year. I wouldn't like to see childer hungry. I'd feel very lonely and sorry for them if they hadn't enough plain food to eat. Plenty of potatoes, vegetables and a bit of meat if they had it. There should be no reason for a child to be hungry nowadays. You can make up a lovely dinner even just with potatoes and some vegetables and a bit of butter . . . and even an egg or two if they had it. That's my idea of life anyways. I always pray to God to help because God is good and he never refuses anybody if we ask him nicely.

Padre Pio was one of Granny Nancy's favourites. A butterfly landed on this picture the day after Granny Nancy passed away.

Why do you believe in God?

Aw he's very good. He never hurts us and he always wants to help us if he can. When I ask him for anything sincerely, he has always given it to me.

I grew up in a family who always had their faith. I guess I must have got my faith from my mam because my dad died young. Bad things have happened in my life and my faith has got me through. When my husband died after the car crash, I had to lean on my faith to get me through because in the end what else do you have. I believed he was gone to heaven and was in a good place with God and all the saints. Otherwise, what else is there really? To think you just end up in the ground and that's it. That's why I believe in God, and I think maybe that's what's gone a bit wrong with the world. Nowadays we have to see everything to believe because with the modern times, you can make any dream a reality. But with God and faith, you can't make it real in any sense, it has to be in your heart and in many ways you have to believe in something nobody can see.

Granny Nancy had a wonderful faith in all the saints and loved celebrating all their special days. This is Granny with her much loved St. Bridget's cross and me too!

Back in your early days Gran, there was a great divide in religions here in Ireland, can you remember anything of that time?

We lived among four families of protestants. You wouldn't believe how good they were to us back then. They would never come without a sugar stick or something for us as kids. They loved the good chat like ourselves. They used to be disappointed if anyone came in and interrupted it. They were lovely people.

Now we don't know what faith anyone is anymore. It's good to have so many choices and it's good it's left up to everyone to have their own way around it all. I would never force my ways, beliefs or opinions on anyone. I think it's great now that we are much more open minded on lots of different issues. Nobody feels left out. It's a different world to what I was brought up but that's progress. One thing for sure, it's great that we are all friends now.

What do you think of priests and the role they have played in your life?

I think they have a hard old life myself. It's a hard choice to make that you are giving up all your life to God and to other people. It's a very selfless act to become a priest. They are great people for doing what they do. It's not easy. It must be very lonely. My faith is very important to me so I'm very grateful for all my priest friends. Fr. John Keegan, a family friend all my life. I knew Fr. John as a child. He lived up the road and I'm so grateful to have him in my life. He is such a good friend to me. And Fr. Gerard Breen. Another great friend to me and he has been so good to me in so many ways. Always bringing me gifts and he's great for saying prayers with me as well. Monsignor Marron was another great man of faith too. He was in this parish and was liked by us all. We were sorry to see him leave but that's the way the church works. Also Fr. Tom Gilroy is our priest in the parish and he does great work. I count myself very lucky to count all priests as my friends.

Do you think priests should be moved around?

I think it's very silly to be moving priests when they are happy in a parish. Of course, I know you can't please everyone in this life but when a priest is happy where he is, you can be nearly guaranteed the parishioners are happy too. I never see sense in moving priests when things are working. As the saying goes, why break what's already working. It's very silly thing to do and also, it's not fair on the priest because then he has to start all over again. And nowadays with so little if anyone taking up the vocation to be a priest, I think common sense would tell you, to keep parishes happy rather than using some old model of shaking things up.

Granny Nancy pictured with Fr. Michael Whittaker, Fr. Michael Kilmartin, Fr. John Keegan and Fr. Gerard Breen at her 106th Birthday Mass held in St. Finian's Church in Clonard, County Meath.

Should priests be allowed get married?

Yes, they should and they should be let live like everyone else. Why wouldn't they? And the nuns as well. That is one aspect that needs to change. Everyone deserves a full chance at happiness if they want it.

What's your favourite prayer?

The 'Hail Holy Queen' is my favourite prayer because it's about the mother of mercy. I also like to say this one before I go to sleep. I say it every single night with all my other prayers. It goes like this, "Here I lay myself down to sleep, I give my soul to God to keep. There are four angels at my bed. St Matthew, Mark Luke and John. If any danger comes to me, Mother Mary, please wake me". I've been saying that prayer since I was a child and that wasn't today or yesterday. Sometimes I get them a bit jumbled up but I have the right heart saying it so I think God is happy enough with that. It gives me great comfort especially all the years I lived on my own after Bob dying. It's not easy adjusting to life on your own but thank God I have. The mind is a great thing, you just have to tell yourself, you can get through this and then one day, you will say to yourself, I've done it. I still miss Bob lots but I'll meet him again when it's my time to leave this earth and I know all will be well again.

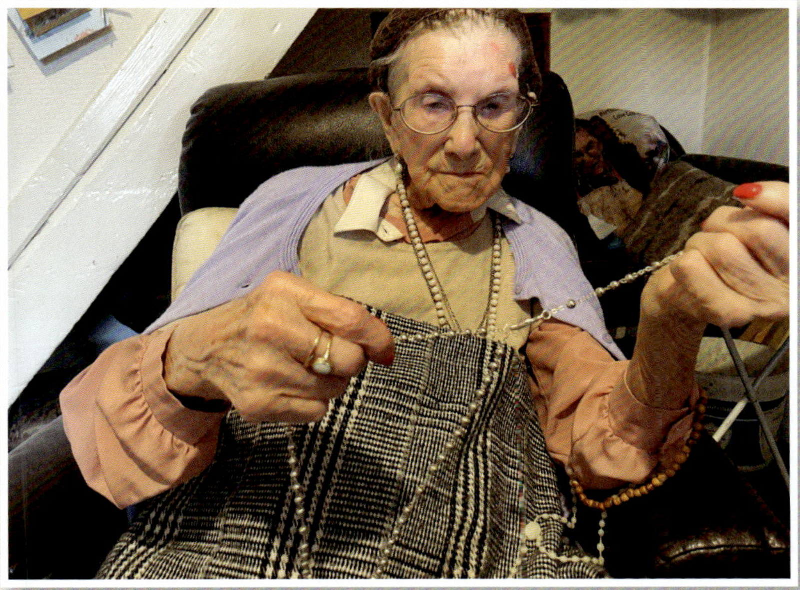

Granny Nancy with her much loved rosary beads.

Do you remember getting your communion or confirmation?
I don't remember too much about it really. I had a white dress with frills for my communion. And the only thing I remember about my confirmation is that if you were good, you got a white ticket. But if you got a red ticket you had to be examined on the day of the confirmation by the bishop. Or maybe it was the other way round. Either ways, I remember it was important you knew your answers when it came to that day!

What does God look like?
I do often think about this Louise. I do see him with his mother and I think God has a beard in my mind. A tall thin strong man. I don't think there's any man like him. Every time I do get a bit of a blink in my eye, I see him.

What do you think Heaven looks like?

I think it's done round with big seats and they are all grandly dressed and we are all talking to one another and praying to each other. When you would sit down here in my armchair and think about what it is like, it's a mystery. Who made it or how did it come around to being? I just believe in God, and I know he won't let me down. I think it's colourful up there. I think it's gold like the tabernacle. Goldish like. Really beautiful. Well, the way they are praying for everyone nowadays we can be sure there is a lovely place in Heaven waiting for us all. Everyone is waiting for us up there. I think they are anyways.

There's no such thing as hell. People were terrified of that long ago. There is no need for that. It did nobody good to be afraid like that. I just want to know if you get something to eat and what's the food like? What do you think Louise?

You know how I love my food. It will be great to meet everyone as well. I wonder what my mother and father will be like. Then there's my brothers Jimmy, John, Mick and my sisters Mag and Bess. And I can't wait to see Bob again and my beautiful daughters the twins, Margaret and Anne. I don't want to think about it in ways and yet I hope it's just like I imagine it to be. I'd love somebody to come back and tell me what's it like. I don't think about it too much if I'm honest. I just hope I go peacefully. My wish would be to slip off in my own bed in my own home and not make any fuss and please God that will be the way, but as we all know, nobody knows. It must be near my time at this stage to go to heaven [as she laughs]. Even God can't believe I'm still here [laughing again]. He mustn't want me yet.

Aw gran I don't think it's near your time at all. Look how healthy you are. Sure you are better than me. Sure you could be living your best life for another ten years or maybe more.

Oh God help you if I am!

You're very easy to mind. Sure I'll mind you for as long as you're here Gran. And as long as we have tea, there won't be a bother on us. Sure we don't know what's ahead of any of us. Will you do me one favour Gran, if you get to heaven before me, will you send me signs, so I know you are there

and I promise if I go before you, I'll send you signs just so we know that each other is safe.

Of course, I will Louise. Sure, I'll be gone before you but I suppose you are right, we never know what God has in store for us. But I promise you, when I get to Heaven, I'll send you signs to let you know I'm there because I know how much I'd like to know what it's like up there. That's a promise so! I suppose you are right Louise about life. We don't know what's in store for any of us and sure we can't control any of it either. I don't know nor you don't know. None of us know. Isn't it great we don't know? Otherwise, we would all be preparing for it. We would be all getting ready if we knew we were going to die. I'd be organising new clothes for the last outing [laughs again]. When we don't know, we don't have to get ready for it isn't that right Louise? I have to be honest I never think of it. And maybe that's what keeps me well.

The sun rising over St. Finian's Cemetery in Clonard, County Meath.

It's all in God's hands isn't it Gran?

You're right Louise. Really none of us know anything about anything in the big scale of things. There's a lot of people who think they know everything nowadays but sure really they know as much as me and you - nothing [a big hearty laugh while saying this]. We don't know anything really. Thank God we don't know. I don't think about dying or any problems really and I think that's what keeps me well. I've no control and thank God I'm not afraid of dying either. When God wants me, he will come take me and until then I'll keep laughing and drinking tea with you Louise in my big armchair. Sure, I couldn't be happier.

I took this photo of myself and Gran in Clonard Church because it reminds me of all the happy times we shared together . . . one of my favourite photos of us together.

So Gran, since we have been locked in, you amazingly have taken to virtual mass like a duck to water. I'm so impressed by how much you have embraced technology to follow mass. What do you make of it all?

I have my bags packed here Louise. Where will we fly today? Egypt I think. I couldn't think of anywhere there now. That's what my messing gets me. Aw no. I think we'll just stay in Ireland will we? I don't think I know anyone in Egypt [as she laughs].

Isn't it great you can get mass anywhere? It's just amazing. Sometimes I can't believe it. And that's the truth. I remember you saying to me at the start of all this Covid thing would I like to look at mass and I said to myself, Louise is gone mad [as she laughs again], and next minute you had me sitting up in front of your computer looking at mass and I hadn't left my kitchen chair. Have you ever heard anything like it? Sure, I couldn't believe it then and I nearly can't believe it now either. Well, I'll tell you something, it saved my life if I'm honest. It's been a God send being able to watch mass all over the country and even all over the world. It's one of the most brilliant things I've seen in all my life. Isn't technology just wonderful? I have to also give a big mention to Radio Maria. I couldn't believe that radio station on the television. When you found that for me Louise, I struck gold as well. Sure Radio Maria is just wonderful company. So many lovely people run it and are involved in it. Sure wasn't I even on it myself a few times. I said the rosary one evening there on it. You and your mam Olive helped me, remember that Louise?

Granny loved having her three rosary beads at all times around her left arm.

I do Gran. I remember it vividly. It was very funny. Because I think we were just meant to be answering Fr. Eamonn as he led it, but you ended up leading it and I remember me and mam trying not to laugh in the middle of it. We looked to each other and just said there is nothing Granny can't do. In the middle of a pandemic, there you were leading a rosary live on the radio and not a bother on you. You even said the last decade in Irish. I'll never forget it Granny. You are some woman for one woman that is for sure!

It was very nice to be asked onto Radio Maria. I really enjoyed it as you know. I have to say all this technology you have introduced me to has been so helpful to me. I really love looking at the masses online. I hope they never stop doing it this way. Because as I've got older, I'm not as able-bodied as I use to be and before covid I loved going to mass but in recent years you wouldn't get me going out in the bad weather and I'm just thinking of all the people who can enjoy mass just like me now because of the computer. Really, I hope we learn from this time. See there are lots of people who might not have anyone to bring them to mass or just might not be able to go for whatever reason, and now this online option will keep the door open for everyone. I just think it's brilliant. I know some of the people who will always give out will say, sure that's not mass at all, you need to be in the church. But as we know there will always be people who will look for the negative. Well, what I think is, if you are making any effort whatsoever, it's your faith that matters not where you are. God doesn't mind where you say your prayers or even if you don't even say prayers. God just loves you talking to him so I definitely wouldn't agree with them on that. Your faith is in your heart. Now I love the church, I think it's a very special place but in the times we are living, this is brilliant. And really this option is brilliant for everyone.

Have you a favourite mass you enjoy Granny?

Well you know me Louise, I'm not a fan of picking favourites! I love them all. And they have all been brilliant. We haven't gone to a mass yet that I said, 'God that's awful boring'. Instead, I think the two of us have been so happy with the standard of lovely homilies the priest's give not to mention the music and the beauty of so many churches. We really have so many lovely talented people and pretty churches in this country. We are so very lucky when you think of all the churches we have. I do love listening to mass from Knock Shrine and Galway Cathedral. Fr. Richard was so kind to mention me a few times in Knock and it's such a special place. I do love Knock. Also Fr. Peter Rabbitte has been so kind to me too. They are two masses we never miss every day aren't they Louise? And then we could mix in anywhere after that. So many lovely people have invited us to their masses and so many priests have been so kind to mention me and you when we look in.

Granny absolutely loved watching mass virtually on my laptop and Gran loved when I bought her a set of headphones as a little treat! "I look very cool don't I Louise?"

Sure where would you get it? I love that you kind of make it a game every day where we go when we are picking a mass. I love that you name loads of counties and then I pick one and then we pick a town or village between us. We have done great driving in our car and sure we have been in every county around the country at this stage. You never take petrol money either [as she laughs] . . . and to think I'm sitting here drinking my tea and watching mass. Again, I can't tell you how much this has meant to me, Louise. I just love looking and listening to mass.

My faith is very important to me. God has never let me down and when things get hard all I can do is pray and then everything comes right again. If you are struggling don't worry, I'll say a prayer for you and everything will be all right . . . and sure if I'm not here in my chair and I'm gone up above, I'll promise to pray for you there. And sure then me and God will watch the masses on our computer together [as she laughs again]. You will have to send me up the internet Louise [laughs again].

Gran loved watching mass on my phone and loved my earphones too. She said she felt very modern watching it on the phone and of course, her favourite part was the cup of tea in her hand.

Granny Nancy loved her comfy armchair by her jubilee stove.

CHAPTER FIVE
GRANNY NANCY & THE PANDEMIC

Myself and Granny enjoying life to the full while the world stood still.

We're in the middle of a lockdown as we chat Granny. What do you make of it all?

It's a strange time to be living. It's a frightful time with this old virus but we will still remember all who are suffering and pray that this old virus will go back to wherever it came from. We can get through anything if we just do what we are told. We can get through this. And in life, all you need to do is believe in God and be kind to each other and you will get through anything.

You don't have to go out to be active. If you're able to get up, just walk through the house. Keep up going around and don't let yourself get stiff. Keep the legs active and make a few pancakes if you have the flour, sugar, and a bit of soda, a drop of milk and an egg and whoever is in the house with you, give them a nudge to help you. It's very important to help each other. Parents and families should try and stay together if they can at all. I think we have to try harder to work out problems in families rather than walking away from each other.

Life is much more complicated it seems nowadays, but really at the end of the day, love and kindness is all we need to show to each other and things can always be worked out. I know that is easier said than done but we must try harder to not give up on each other. It's good to help each other and you will always feel good helping someone else. Don't forget kindness is always the winner.

This photo I took as we recorded our little dancing clip for Luan Parle's music video. We laughed and laughed and Gran said "Can you believe a young one like me is going to be in a music video?" We definitely tried to find fun in the very quiet days of lockdown.

Are you lonely being locked in? Do you miss all your visitors?

It's very lonesome because of this virus, I have nobody coming in and out like I used to. It all changed overnight. All my life my home has been a place of visitors, family and friends and I miss them so very much. I've always believed that a home is not for show nor is it something to be kept perfect. Instead, I believe it's a place where you can share with the people you love. My friends and neighbours are so important to me and my family so I miss them all a lot but I'm adjusting to the situation and please God we will be out of this soon if everyone does what they are told. Only the special people can get in and they are very few.

The days are long in their own way but I'm so lucky to be well and to be at home. I got a present of a jigsaw and it has put me in great humour altogether from a lovely girl, one of your friends Louise, wasn't it? Because I'll tell you girls, the little pieces weren't as big as the nail on your finger, and you would want to be a genius to make it. But no better woman to try it out. I've nearly it done now with a little help from a few helping hands, and I'll have it hanging on the wall when this old thing is gone. And then people will say who did that and I'll say proudly I did it and you done it and we will all just laugh. And imagine I didn't have to hand out a penny to anyone for these wonderful things. Imagine people are so good to me and they are always thinking of me. I feel so lucky and so grateful for so many lovely people in my life.

Granny Nancy is met with a standing ovation at her 106th birthday mass in October 2019.

Do you think the pandemic will bring people closer together?

I hope it will make families more attached to each other. I hope it does anyway. If this doesn't, nothing will. Maybe people might pick up their faith again too. It was getting very low in this country before this but please God people will see the goodness in saying a prayer or even asking God to help them when they are in need. People weren't going to mass before this really. Confessions were forgotten really too. In the last ten to fifteen years people have lost their faith. Families should try and stay together. And not want everything to be perfect or push to have everything. We should always help each other out and reach towards each other too. The effects of this virus might move people together once we come out the other side. I keep hoping people will learn from this time of us being separated that life is fragile and we should always make an effort with each other. I'll keep saying my Hail Marys, the Hail Holy Queen, the Creed and the Confiteor. I'll keep saying them to myself, but I'll say them for everyone and we'll soon be out of it all please God.

Do you think anything will be learned from this time?

Some of them will learn nothing because they wouldn't listen to you no matter what happens in life. I do hope they all remember the hardship of it though. It wasn't easy to sit and not go anywhere. I hope one thing is learned or how would I say it, I hope carers get the recognition and rewards and appreciation they deserve after this awful time. The carers were brilliant to me and always have been and not forgetting you Louise. I've no words for them all. They never took a day off.

I'm so lucky to have such gorgeous people in my life. They are all my friends and I hope I'm their friend too. I hope the government learn to appreciate all these wonderful people minding us older people and the job they do for us. They don't get half enough money and I hope after the virus calms down the role of a carer is put up there on the top. Without them we would be all lost at home and not to forget no matter the weather nor this old thing, they never missed a day. I hope we learn to appreciate the carers and all the work they do to help us live in our homes. Louise, I'd be lost without you here in the house. All of ye deserve so much because nobody should ever be taken from their home unless they want to leave. I'm so lucky to live and please God die in my home and to be honest everyone should have the same opportunity as me whether you are young, old or even one hundred and seven years of age.

You're such a calm and serene person granny, how do you manage to be so happy?

I'm very content and happy. I'd stay here all-day saying prayers. My family are always coming in and out which has played a big part in me staying so well. I have a wonderful family and I hope they know how important they are to me. My daughters, my son, my nieces and nephews, my cousins, grandchildren, great-grandchildren, great-great grandchildren and so many wonderful friends. I just love to see them all and really, they have kept me so content and brought me so much happiness down through all the years. We never have an angry word between us. We are so happy together. The blessed mother keeps me so happy and well, to have helped me live my whole life in my own home.

I have a huge array of friends and family, too many to name but they all know who they are. When this started, I had to cut down on them all which broke my heart but thank God for the phone. Hopefully this will all be over soon so I can see them all again. I miss them all dearly.

Granny Nancy pictured with all her children, grandchildren, great-grandchildren and great-great grandchildren on her 100th Birthday.

What helps you get through this time or is there any tip you would give someone to break the day up if they were fed up?

I love my mug of tea here on my knee taking a good sip out of it. Tea means a lot to me. I actually think it has got me through a lot of bother in my life. The day can be very long and even in my younger days whether it was a problem I couldn't figure out or if I felt the time was going slow, I'd always make myself a cup of tea. I love the tea you see and it's never let me down. Barry's tea all my life as long as I can remember. By the time the kettle was boiled or if I was walking around with it in my hand, I'd either figure out my problem or have forgotten what I was worrying about so either way it was great. I think making a cup of tea is the answer to any problem you might have or if you're struggling with the slowness of the day or night come to think of it. I'd often make tea in the middle of the night. If you can't sleep, just get up and make yourself a cup of tea. I promise you will feel the better of it and you will love to get back into your bed then.

I love the tea bags myself. They are so handy compared to the old days of loose tea. The first time it came out, we got the Barry's. But I know there are old women who go to the loose tea still. It's whatever you like yourself. If I had to drink the loose tea, I'd drink it. Like if there was nothing else only loose tea. If I was compelled to it, I'd buy it but I do love the Barry's tea bags. They are very clean and it's tasty. There is no tea leaves everywhere you go. Aren't I right? And I just love a day like today, here lying back on my sofa, drinking my tea, talking to my grandchild, my lady of the house, my best friend. Sure what more would you want in life?

It's the simple things Louise, never forget that, it's the simple things. You mind me all the time and you stay with me all the time at night and in the day Louise and sure we love our tea together too. I'd be lost without you and I wouldn't be here for sure only for you. Our time together has flown, hasn't it? I hear you peeping in at night at me but I don't let on I see you! I'd see your shadow but it's such comfort to have you. You tip in on your toes. I'd hear you but I would pretend I am asleep. You would be so neat and tidy and silent looking in on me. We're the best of friends. We are so lucky to get on so well. And you cover me up so nice in bed and our cups of tea, sure I couldn't be happier!

Gran loved flowers so every so often I would buy her a bunch as a little surprise. I would always say to her, you are my little flower Gran and she would smile, and say "No Louise you are mine". I miss my little flower every day x

What do you think of the Covid19 virus?

I've never seen anything like it. Even if there were flu's back in my young days, it was never so severe as this. There wasn't a thing about masks then. You just wouldn't visit someone if they were very sick to give them a chance to get better. You could die from the flu back then. You might leave biscuits or a cake outside someone's door and if they weren't too sick you would offer to try to mind them. With this virus, it was a different story altogether. Nothing in the past was as severe as we have felt with this virus though. It's very scary as it travelled all over the world the way it did this time. This virus moved because nowadays people move a lot. The people who move a lot nowadays on holidays, sometimes they are people just showing off because they feel they need to go on holidays three four times a year. Nobody ever needed to leave home that often in the old days. I think we might have been poorer back then, but I think we were happier in many ways. And our homes were places we felt safe and really you didn't even think about heading off anywhere. It's all so different now. I think all this travelling sometimes is all a bit for show. One person says to another I was here or there or wherever and then the next person thinks they have to go now too. It's a bit silly really. I know it's nice to go away for a few days but I think we've lost the run of ourselves a bit with travel. No wonder this virus came the way it did. But it slowed us all down didn't it and maybe that's not all bad. Sure can't you get everything you love here in Ireland. We live in a beautiful country. And it's good to spend your time off and your money in your own country and locally too. Ireland is a great country. We have everything anyone would dream of. I couldn't be happier. I love where I live and all the lovely people. You wouldn't get me on a plane that's for sure . . . Well only if we were going to mass on the computer of course Louise [as she laughs].

Gran was a wonderful lady for common sense and foresight and was very supportive of mask-wearing as it kept us all safe.

What do you think of the mask?

I think it's a very important part of preventing the virus from getting in on us. My family and my carers have always worn their masks and thank God the virus never got into my home because they were so good to wear their masks from the start. My granddaughter Louise completely believes in the wearing of the mask from the minute this started, and she was right in her thinking. The mask is very important and it's hard to understand why someone wouldn't wear it. There are some people very ignorant. They think they won't get it. But they will probably end up giving it to you and me, and all those of us who are following the rules. That's when things get messy. When people don't protect each other. It's always the way when people think they are better than the rules. But we must just keep doing the right thing because then others will feel confident to do the right thing too. It's all about trying to do your best and also trying to keep others safe as well.

For me, it's common sense to wear a mask and sure they are so cheap there is no reason you aren't wearing a mask when you meet your friends. It seems no matter how much people think they are smart with all these gadgets, I nearly think they aren't so smart at all. But luckily that's just a few.

Granny loved her landline telephone and LOVED to call her friends and family and loved when they called her too. I took this photo as she was being interviewed by the lovely Mairead Ronan on Today FM for her birthday. Mairead, you can see she loved chatting to you too!

This is not your first pandemic Gran. You were only a little girl when the Spanish flu was rampant and that pandemic was severe. So here you are in a second pandemic and you are inspiring everyone to keep positive as best we can. Does this compare to hard times you've been through before?

This has been the worse I ever heard of in that we can't see anyone. It's nearly worse than the wars really because even when there were wars, we could still see our family and our neighbours. It came so much to Ireland didn't it this old virus. It went through every county and every village and even every country. When the wars happened it wasn't like that. We knew they were happening, but every home wasn't affected the same way we are with this. Now I'm not saying the wars weren't bad, but it was a different feeling if that makes sense. You would hope we won't see any more wars in our lifetimes. The least people can do now that we are so well educated is not fight with each other, but I guess it's not about education, it's about power and people wanting to be better than others. All the schools are closed with the virus out there. I don't even remember school being closed in the wartimes.

How did you find the rolling precaution of lockdowns? You've been cocooned the whole time with me and other family members and the carers, so it's been very tough on you Gran. When the lockdowns were lifted, we kept cocooning just to be extra safe but I know none of this is easy on you.

I was very lonely I'll tell you the truth at the start. I really didn't like the idea of the lockdowns or the way everyone was just cut off. I missed my friends and family coming in the door. I've never had to close my door to anyone in all my lifetime and that's a long time with my door open. But it was the right thing to do to control that bad old virus moving around. We just had to put down our heads and get on with it. Thank God it seems a bit better now and in time please God we will get a better handle on it and a vaccine will be found. If it was over and gone, it would be great, but you don't know where it is still, so we have to be careful and vigilant. And I don't mind that, because I don't want it and I don't want you to get it or anyone I love and that's as simple as that. I don't mind being patient and waiting for things to be good again. All my friends and family will be waiting for me, and I'll be waiting for them. Thank God for the phone and sure you with that video calling Louise we have great gas altogether. I'm lucky I have you in here. Sure, look at us now having the chats. If the covid didn't come I couldn't have told anyone my life story [as she laughs out loud]. We must have it nearly written now do we [laughing to herself again].

I was thrilled when 'The Irish Independent' published my piece about the joy I was having in living and cocooning with Granny. I was so glad I got to archive our relationship in a very special way.

While filling in time in lockdown, me and Gran did lots of home schooling and Granny really loved the hand writing games.

CHAPTER SIX

GRANNY NANCY'S THOUGHTS ABOUT HERSELF

Did you ever think you would live to be 107?

No, I don't ever remember coming to this age. I never remember the years coming up on me if that makes sense. Or even here sitting, I don't even feel I'm 107. It doesn't feel that long. God love those younger than me and not able to get out of bed. Thank God I'm well and able. I have a lovely clean house, a lovely clean kitchen and a lovely clean cooker. I love that they got my house painted for me when I broke my hip so it's looking great in here. And sure, I don't look half bad either. They tell me I don't look my age. Maybe they are messing. But I definitely don't feel it.

Gran loved all her presents she received for her 107th birthday. Everyone was so kind. She is pictured here with this beautiful framed picture from San Connolly.

What age do you feel?

I feel like seventy or so. I don't want to dress in old-fashioned clothes because I don't feel my age. Some days I feel seventy and then other days I feel only sixty. I've great health all my life. Just my bad eye was the biggest thing I had a problem with and that was from the accident and breaking my hip when I was one hundred and five. I'm not in any pain and I've a great ability in my body. Aren't I a terrible lucky woman that I've never been sick really? I never had a serious sickness. People half my age could get a fall and would have a broken hip forever and they would never have recovered. I never felt I was burdened with pain, I'm very lucky. Great limbs God must have given me. It wasn't from idleness anyways. I had to work hard in my younger days with six of them going to school. Aww, it's all good. It's all done. I'm having a lady's life now. Only for my grandchild Louise, she stayed with me. I'll never forget that. I'm blessed with such good family. I've so many of them taking care of me all my life. I have to admit I am looking forward to my friends, my neighbours and all my family coming back to visit me when this virus is over.

RTE's Ciaran Mullooly interviewing Granny on her 107th birthday at her home in Clonard in October 2020 along with Jimmy Norman on camera. So grateful to Ciaran and Jimmy for all their help in spreading the good news of Granny Nancy throughout the years.

Your skin? How is it so good?

I never do much with it. Oil of Olay is the answer to good skin. In the morning I do my face after my breakfast. When I sit out in the kitchen I just rub it on, leave it on for a few minutes and then wipe it off with a tissue.

If I was going somewhere I might put a little bit on my face but that's all I do with my skin. I have to be honest some nights I might be feeling tired, but I still do it because it's a habit and part of my routine. But don't worry if you forget, get yourself a cup of tea and a bit of sugar and that would be good for your skin too. I use hand cream every evening. Since I stopped working, I put on hand cream as it keeps my skin soft and in good condition. If someone gave me, it as a gift when I was working I would never use it and now I love it.

Granny was just so lovely to look at and I'm so grateful I took so many photos of her. Her beautiful skin was one of her many famous attractions to so many. Oh and that cute little smile!

Your hair is not grey Granny. Have you some special trick that has kept your hair so good after one hundred and seven years?

Imagine only once in my life did, I ever get a colour. Teresa started over at the jet in the village there, to do hairdressing. I went over there and got a perm and a colour, but I wasn't grey. I just got it done because it was the fashion, and everyone was doing it. It was a new trend and there was so much fuss about this idea of changing the colour of your hair, I said I'd try it out. I suppose I was about forty years of age, so it wasn't today or yesterday.

But would you believe I've never got a colour since that day. In the beginning, it was dear enough to get a perm and colour. I used to get it washed and set from there on out. I never went grey or white, so I never bothered with the colour end of things. I'm not sure how I was so lucky to never go grey really.

How are your eyes?

They are good today. I don't need the tea bags. You know some days they do need a bit of extra attention but today they are good. One question I do have though is, why do they make the top of the eye drops so small? That tiny lid is no benefit for the older people you know. The older people are not thought of. They forget they can be so helpless. When they are well themselves, they forget and don't think about how it feels to be old.

Are you lucky?

I am to be so well and nearly all the family have good health. None of them have a serious sickness thank God. If you are not active, then you will nearly always get sick. It's good to be busy. If you keep active, you will keep well. And I just mean getting up and pottering around the house. And of course, the same goes for your mind, if you don't keep that active and keep mixing with people, your head will get bothered as well.

Granny loved all her family. Pictured here are her grandchildren Marie Boyd, Grainne Maye, Claire Coghlan and myself as Gran turned 103 years young.

It was a very special moment for Granny when we lined out her seven presidential medals on her 107th birthday in her beautiful cosy home in Clonard.

CHAPTER SEVEN

GRANNY NANCY AND CURRENT AFFAIRS

Gran happy to have done her duty and voted in Clonard National School.

What do you think about how the country is run nowadays?

Well, I think they are not doing enough for the people they should be doing it for especially for the homeless and the childer that are not looked after. They should look after the vulnerable first and foremost. Also, they need to take better care of the elderly as well. I know I'm one of the lucky ones but not everyone is as lucky as me. They have the way, and they have the money, so they should mind the people who need minding.

Do they waste money?

They don't spend it on the people who really need it so yes, I would say they waste a good bit of it if I'm honest. I know some might think it's easy for me to give out at my stage of my life and it's always easy to find faults when you're not doing the job yourself, but I've seen them all go through at this stage. I saw what we went through to have our own independence, so I value all that was fought for, and I love our little country. I just think we could be doing much better with the amounts of money we do hear them talk about. Millions here, billions there. They need to give out good housing and make it a thing of the past to be homeless in this country. Imagine we had no money back when I was growing up yet there was no such thing as homeless people, and now that we have money, endless amount of it, I've never heard so many people homeless. There is no sense in that. Houses can be erected easy nowadays. Not swanky houses, just comfortable houses. Give them comfortable homes. In my young days we called them the cottages and they were very lovely and handsome homes and then the people did them up more as they got money themselves.

But the politicians have the money now and they're not spending it properly. They all have money to spend. They do a lot of talking about it don't they Louise? Let them talk right. There is no use them talking if they are not doing anything. I'm sitting here in a chair looking at them on the television there in the Dail when they should be out working and helping the poor people. I don't mind a certain amount of talk, nothing wrong with that but when the talk is not followed by actions, well then you just lose everyone's trust. They don't know what it is to be poor. They never knew. But get on their feet now and do something for the poor and for anyone who needs their help. All they do nowadays is talk. There is no sense that there are homeless people in this country. There's plenty of money but it looks like they don't know how to manage money or worse still are spending it wastefully.

Does too much money change people and in this instance politics?
Oh, why wouldn't it. If you or I had too much money, we would spend it fairly quick if we had it. But these people know there are poor people and lots struggling, and they can help them so it shouldn't be too hard. Getting the money in life is the hardest part, helping people is the easy part if you ask me.

Come on don't bring me out of my chair to have to follow you about because I know plenty of people we could help. It's not their money to be wasting either which is worse. It was given to them by all the hard-working people of this country. I'll soon tell them if they come for their vote, it's not your money to squander. Nowadays people seem to not have value on money if they can get it easy and worse still if it's not yours to earn, it seems to just disappear.

What do you think of all the scandals?
They should be ashamed of themselves having us listening to them. The poor people wanting a little and they can't get anything. And then you have the people who are paid to mind our money, and they are out squandering it and enjoying it on themselves. Come on now boys come out and open your mouths and hands and get to the poor. I'm not asking you for anything. But I'm asking for those who need it badly. I'll follow you up until it's done because it's not fair to waste so many millions. I hear it on the radio all the time. I'm sitting here quite happy, an old woman. I haven't a terrible lot of grandeur but am very comfortable. But I like to see everyone with a nice comfortable kitchen, fireplace and firing and helping the little childer to be chatting and comfortable. Thank you, politicians. You know how to carry on if you put your mind to it. Everyone deserves to have a home, and nobody should be homeless in this country. And don't be delaying or you'll have me after you. I'm well able to talk and fight for those who need to be heard. I know lots are trying their best but it's not good enough.

Do you think we need change in politics?
Yes, we do need different parties. Change is happening now. We can see it in the last few elections. People are not happy how things are going,

and they are beginning to voice how they feel at the voting box. And that's the place to voice it if you ask me. And that's because the money is being spent badly and the people on the ground can see it and they feel it. Sometimes change is what you need in a situation. We need new people in there to push them on. New eyes on everything. Let them young people in there too because they are the next generation.

And not forgetting the women. Come on the women. So much money spent wrongly and not wisely so go back now and help who you should help. The homeless. The childer. And the hardworking people. We need fresh new people who won't be spending all the money on themselves. I'm not looking for anything. I'm getting enough myself. Thank God for my family, my childer and my grandchildren around me to help me. I'm not looking to the government at all. I'm quite happy and I want the rest of the people to get into my position and get happy. And get a little house with three or four rooms, with whatever amount they need and whatever amount of childer they have. Some might have three or four. Others might have only two or none at all. Let them be able to buy or build a house to their means. Everyone should be able to have a home of their own. Everyone should be proud as punch of their own home. I don't know who punch was [laughs to herself].

Granny was very passionate about her right to vote and became a famous voice on the television and radio encouraging people to get out and vote and how she remembered when women didn't have a vote.

They need new people, and they need someone to direct them. They need to listen to them. We don't need big words and big talk. Just need to keep it simple. Everything is very expensive nowadays and that's not good. We have millions of euros, and they are just not spending it in the right way. They are helping themselves too much. They are giving it to the rich rather than the poor. I'd love them to get new people in to direct them in the right way not wasting money.

What do you think of the new children's hospital being built and where it's located Gran? I know you have strong thoughts on this.

Tell me this Louise, I just can't understand that million or even billions of euros being spent on the country children's hospital in the middle of Dublin City. Why would you put it in the middle of Dublin City? Who does that hospital suit? Nobody only people who are not too far away. Couldn't they have built it in the midlands where everyone can attend it. That would have made sense. Thank God I've been very lucky that I got great attention, but I never was in hospital for too long thank god. The few times I was in it I got on very good. The hospitals seem to have declined by what I'm listening to on the radio here. They are not looking after the people half as good as they use to. Hearing people falling out of beds and just awful stories. It's terrible. Look after the people who are really sick and that need the help. No point looking after me. I'm happy but everyone deserves help when they need it. I'm listening to everything, and I'll make them move. I know the staff are working so hard but it's such a mess, isn't it? All you have to do is listen to the news for five minutes and all you hear is problem after problem . . . and everyone giving out about services and staff worn out . . . There was no money in our years but they were all very well looked after when it came to the time. I don't remember ever being without anything. Now the young childer are in bother. The older people can't get carers or attention without a fight. We need to have hospitals and services that can mind the people. Sure, if we don't have that, what are we at as a country.

You were out voting recently in the general election before Covid landed. Voting is very important to you isn't its Gran?

I did my vote. I was happy to do it. I'm sorry to say I don't really know who's running the country. They are arguing about different things on the radio and are not willing to go into government together now that we have voted. They'll have to fix it up themselves. I can't do no more. Once is enough. It's very silly. They should be able to sit down and talk it over and work together as parties. And if they want to go with each other, well then do. They have to work together on this. They are not going to figure it out the way they are going on. One lad there and another lad beyond in Tullamore. It's important to respect what people vote for. They are not paying enough attention to what the people are saying. They are having it their own way. None of the parties got enough to be on their own, but it's not a bad thing to learn how to work together. Even if new parties want to get involved, you would have to open your mind to all choices nowadays. You can't be looking back to root up problems in the past of anyone never mind a party. No matter how good you are, if you want to find problems in someone's past you will find it. But we aren't and don't want to live in the past, it's today that matters. The world has moved on and we as people have to move on as well.

Gran holding her polling card in February 2019. This was Granny's last time to vote and had never missed a vote up to that. "It's our duty to each other and our country to cast our votes on polling day."

Today's problems are all that matters and the focus should always be to try and improve things for everyone and to have kind words, not ugly words to each other.

I really enjoyed my day out voting. I could hardly see everyone who was talking to me. It was a great day. It was lovely talking to my friend Ciaran. He's very good for always coming to see me.

Myself and Gran used to watch the Dail in action on the television and Gran was always very happy to see women being represented in politics.

What do you think of Mary Lou McDonnell?

She's talking a lot of sense. I like her. She is very good. At least she wants to do good for the poor and the homeless. Sinn Fein had a bad name a long time ago but that's what I mean, it's in the past. We can't hold forever what is in the past. Things change, people change, and you should always give people the benefit of the doubt and give everyone a chance. I like Mary Lou. She speaks a lot of sense and anyone who speaks out for the poor and the struggling, will win the interest of the people and of me. She rang me for my birthday when I was one hundred and seven and that was very kind of her. You would be surprised by people. Those you expect can often let you down and those you might not expect surprise you in the best possible way. She was a really lovely person on the phone and now when I see her on the television, I say I know that woman. And that too is very important. Up the women. More women need to be in politics. Men are brilliant but they need us women to balance things out.

I'm still waiting for the president to ring me. He sends me letters but no phone call. I even rang Aras on Uachtarain myself to see would he talk to me or even ring me, but no sound yet. He can't say he doesn't know me; sure he's sent me seven letters.

You make a great old day out when you go voting. It's like a celebration for you isn't it Granny?

Whatever length I'm going to live, I'll just try to do the best I can and of course keep voting as long as I'm here too. A good piece of advice is to keep my mouth shut when necessary and I'll open it well when I have to. I'm in good health thank God and it's great I'm able to talk about so many things and I love going out to vote. It's our duty as people of this country to turn up and vote. Whether you like the people running or not, everyone deserves a chance, and we can't complain about the country if you don't vote.

I love getting dressed up and going down to the local school in Clonard and voting. It's always a great day out. You Louise and your Mam always come with me and sure we make a day out of it. They must all know we went to The Monastery Inn in the village for ice cream as loads of people told me they knew I was there. They are all asking me about my sherry trifle. They are so nice to me down there and we got it on the house. Such a treat. I'm so lucky wherever I go, people are always so nice to me. The world is full of nice people. All I do is smile and I love meeting everyone. It's so easy to be nice. And you will never regret being nice in this world. You never know what someone is carrying in this life, and your smile or kind word could just be what they need.

This photo was taken in the Monastery Inn, Clonard after Gran had cast her vote in the local school. Gran loved a treat and as we used to say together "Don't we deserve it? We sure do."

Granny loved RTE's Ciaran Mullooly and camera man Jimmy Norman visiting Clonard as Gran cast her vote in the elections over the years. Myself and Mam are pictured here also.

CHAPTER EIGHT

GRANNY NANCY'S THOUGHTS ON LOTS OF TOPICS

Myself and Gran pictured in St. Finian's Church in Clonard and God loved how we even had a giggle there.

What do you think about so many people being homeless in Ireland?

The government aren't looking after the homeless. It's a d sgrace. They are wasting the money. Too many big wages for themselves. I heard the government gave themselves a raise in their wages there a while ago. If they spent half that money on houses, we wouldn't have any homeless here. They increase their wages but don't increase the poor people's money. There are childer poor still. People are kind of proud now and they don't want to let on. It's not right. There is so much money in the country and we still have homeless people. It's a shame for the government.

If I was to mention the word 'money', what would you think?

It's good enough If you work it right. It doesn't solve everything, but it helps to have enough. And then if you start fighting with the family about money, you're lost. If the family start fighting, it rises into rows and that's not good. Money is not worth a thing if you don't have your health or your family or friends around you.

Could you give me your thoughts about the older people back in the day?
Long time ago, the old people were all too poor and would be left in all sorts of conditions. So often they were cross as well but I hope nowadays us older people [as she winks] are happier and therefore less cross. I don't think it was their fault back in the day that they were cross. Times were hard and things were often tough, so I guess that's why they ended up being cranky. Thank God nowadays there is no need to be cross. We have everything. But often even if you have everything, you see a lot of people with cross faces [winks again].

What do you think of your carers?
They are so good to me. I love them all. I'd be lost without them. Everyone deserves the care I've received. I love that they all have different personalities. I feel so happy seeing them come in the door and they know me so well. They treat me like their own granny, and I treat them like family. I could say so much about them, but I think they know how I feel about them all. I'll never forget all they have done for me. And I ll always have them in my prayers.

We had so much fun baking and I just loved Gran putting on her special aprons for the occasion.

Myself and Gran spent a lot of time baking during the lockdowns and to say Granny enjoyed it would nearly be an understatement. We both loved baking together and one ingredient that was always present - laughter . . . loads and loads of laughter.

How do you make a wheaten cake?
Well, first you need half flour and half wheaten meal to get the process going. You also will need bread soda. When mixing the two flours you need to make sure you put in the bread soda through a sieve and make sure it doesn't crimp up. Sometimes people would put a spoonful of sugar at this point too, if you wanted sweeten bread. Which is also very nice, but I don't often do that. Then you put in the buttermilk. Keep it stirred till it gets fairly dried up. Then into the oven for an hour till it was baked. I only had the solid fuel cooker back then in the olden days. I

still have it [as she laughs]. We didn't realise how hard it was back then you know as everyone was baking the same way. We only had the solid fuel, and we were so grateful for them. I prefer the easy days [laughing again]. It's nice to be able to enjoy life. I'm enjoying my life immensely. Thanks to them all minding me. I'm so happy and now me and you can bake together Louise and have so much fun. We've done some amount of baking in the last week or two. Scones, brown and white soda bread, you name it, we've made it. No pressure on us, only lots of laughing to see if we burn the cake or if it's raw in the middle [laughs out loud].

What is Happiness?

Happiness for me is not to be worrying about everything. To let it rectify itself. Don't be worrying if you're listening to me now. Whatever you are worrying about, I promise you, it either won't happen or you will have the strength to get through it and out the other side.

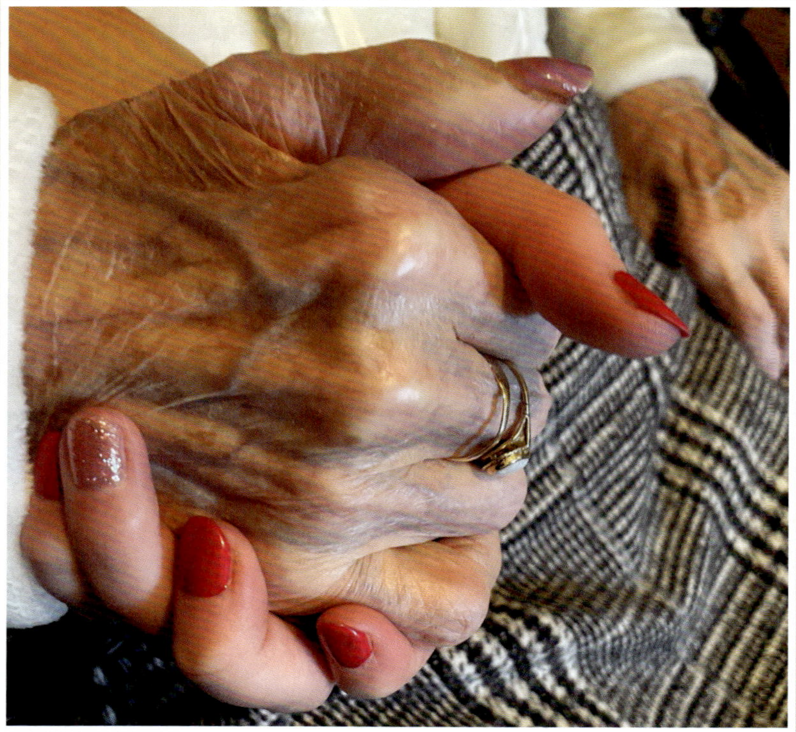

I loved holding your hand Gran. I'll always miss that x

You're very healthy and very happy aren't you Granny?

I count myself terrible healthy Louise. Imagine I've not a pain or an ache. No operations apart from the auld hip that time. I was just after turning 105 and sure didn't I slip and break a bone in my hip. And to add to it, it all happened on Christmas Eve so very eventful altogether. Thank God I got surgery that night in Tullamore Hospital. I got a gamma nail put in. They were a bit anxious of my age especially on Christmas Eve, but I told them I only feel like seventy so don't be worrying about my age. I helped the surgeon to feel happy doing it and in I went. Hours later after lots of noise I have to admit, he had put a gamma nail to secure my hip. I was awake for it all. And sure after a few weeks I was flying up and down the halls on my zimmer frame.

Thank God I never looked back, and after a few more weeks, I was back in my own home here with you and sure you wouldn't even know anything had happened. Even the auld hip didn't hurt me thank God. I was very lucky. God is very happy with me, I think. He must be because he doesn't make me suffer. I smile a lot thank God. I give a lot of money for the poor hungry childer in this country and around the world.

It's nice to be able to help other people. You are very charitable yourself Louise. You give all your money away. You are very good to everyone. Sure, you are always bringing me in stuff, whether treats or little presents. Sure, you mustn't have a penny yourself. I remember people back in the days that wouldn't spend a penny, not like you. They would just save and save. They'd be going round houses eating them out of house and home rather than spending their own. You have to earn money to appreciate it, that's what I always say but there's no point not sharing it either.

What do you think of nursing homes taking care of the elderly?

They are all right and nice if you aren't too sick. You would want to be young and able in there. Actually, if you are good in the mind and able, stay at home and get someone to help you.

You didn't always have electricity did you gran?

It's nearly hard to believe it now Louise but you are right, there was a time when everything wasn't just a switch away. Nowadays it's a switch for this and a switch for that. It's such an easy life really to what I had, so I guess that's why I'm so happy. Switch on the telly. Switch on the radio.

Switch on the heating. Switch on the washing machine. Sure, if you were to tell me this back in the day, I'd have told you, you were mad. Imagine Louise we use to have to go to Callaghy's the local shop which was a good bit down the road in the evening to get paraffin oil. It was hard going back then. We had a big range there and it would eat up the fuel. Oh, I loved my jubilee then and I love it even more now. It's a gift. You wouldn't get one like it nowadays. It was well-minded, and it has never let me down. It's important to mind things. It pays off to mind things and equally to mind people. Did you get anything to eat at all Louise? I did gran. Make sure you mind yourself. You make lovely cups of tea Louise with love in the cup. I was very lucky to get you.

How do you think the elderly are treated in Ireland?

Well enough if they are able to help themselves. If you are looking for help you will have to be able to fight for it. Thank God, Nancy is here and she's better than the queen. I have the best of carers and I'm so lucky. I get on well with them and they get on well with me. They tell me they look forward to coming to me, I think I might be one of their favourites even though I know they don't have favourites . . . But I might be, you would never know. We have many great laughs together. They are so very good to me, and I'll never be able to repay them.

Do you think we shop too much?

We do. There is some that wouldn't buy enough to feed themselves. But they will come into your house and my house to get tea and food. They are that mean that they wouldn't spend their own money on the necessities on themselves. Back in my younger days, those same ones were around then as well so they have always been around. They were educated back then as well, and they wouldn't spend a penny. There is nothing annoys me more than people who won't spend money. What are they going to do with it? Bring it to their grave and put it in their pockets. Two people I knew back in the day would call to me and they had plenty of money, but they come to us and eat us out of house and home. And wouldn't bring a thing with them. I remember a few of them sort came to our home when we were children and my mother would put down a small dinner in front of them, just on purpose because we all were annoyed with them. Nobody likes people who are tight and are counting their pennies. Money is for spending and particularly if you can spend a bit of it on others. We only need so much to live and then the rest is for spending. And if you can give a little bit of it away as well, that's the best bit. It's in sharing that you value what you have. By sharing you recognise that not everyone is as fortunate as ourselves and I always say once I have enough for a bit of food and my bills then, I'll spend and share the rest of what I have left.

What's your favourite day of the week?

Friday because it's pension day. Me and you have a great giggle when it comes to Friday don't we Louise? It's our favourite day together I think. I came up with the mad ideas and Gran's response always was the same, "Count me in. What are we doing? Are we dressing up? Where's your phone?"

This photo was taken as part of the fundraiser I organised for Daffodil Day in aid of cancer support services.

What does your pension mean to you?

Oh, it's lovely. I wouldn't have much without it. Oh lord, it was a big deal when I got it. It was like winning the lottery. Anyone you would meet would be thrilled to be getting it. On thinking about the pension, I've just thought of a story from my much younger days. There was an old woman around the area, and she lived with her brother when I was small.

We would drop her pension to her. Either me or my sister Mag would drop it into her. She would always give us a silver tuppeny bit or a six pence from her pension which was very generous. The old age pension was only five shillings back then. She was awful kind to us.

What did you do with your money from the lady?
There was a shop going to school and we would keep it for that. They sold sugar sticks, and we could buy them with our little money. The Murray's and the boys who would live around there would come with us. We could share it then with them and it was even more enjoyable. We would break it, crack it up and then share it out among ourselves. We nearly always bought a sugar stick from Fosters Shop. They were protestants. On the road from our house to Ardenew. Near the four roads. There were a whole lot of different sugar sticks back then and you could get three sweets a penny. If you had a penny you were made up. They had everything else in that shop too for grown-ups like tea, sugar, flour and groceries. It was a great shop. Sometimes you would get to pick sweets from a jar, and there would be sweets with no wrappers. The dearer sweets always had wrappers.

Did you buy your sweets before or after school?
It would depend on what was for your lunch.

What was your lunch going to school?
Bread and jam were all we had for lunch. No ham or anything fancy like that.

Was knitting popular back then?
Oh god yes, we all did a terrible lot of knitting that time. The wool was cheap. We knitted clothes of all types. They would last the test of time too. Lovely garments really. They went from me to you and the next one down. Not like these days, where you buy something new every week. And everything goes in the bin from last week.

What was your favourite treat?
An egg flip.
Do you remember going dancing?
We used to go to Raharney or Killucan for dancing which wasn't too far away. I was a good dancer [as she laughs]. It was a real old-fashioned

place not done up well. But we loved it. As long as we got in the door. It was only 6 pence or a shilling at the most. There was a selection of different musicians playing. One would be playing the melodeon, another with a mouth organ and then someone playing the fiddle. They made up a band with any auld instruments. Then later on in years, they got much fancier.

Do you remember getting your first car?
It was an auld black van. We were the only ones with one on this road. We used to go to Edenderry on a pony and trap before that. Then we got the van, and we would do the shopping for everyone along the road. It became a weekly trip. They would want stuff they couldn't carry on a bike. Items such as potatoes, vegetables and even bags of coal. See there was no such thing as briquettes back then. There was good coal and bad coal then. Big pieces and small pieces. Slack coal was cheaper for people who didn't have much money.

Only for the car, we would have all been lost. What a treat it was compared to being on our bikes.

Gran was brilliant with trying our technology and always embraced anything I would suggest. "Do you want to try my AirPods Gran?". . . "Oh yep, I'll have a go at them." One of the many reasons, Gran was so happy was her open mind and heart to change with new things.

Can you describe your memory of going into Edenderry shopping on a Saturday back in your younger days?

Edenderry was a great town to shop in and get all you needed. It was a vibrant town with lots going on. So many businesses and they were all as nice as the next one. O'Brien's Grocery was the place we all went as our first stop. The shopping list consisted of bacon and rashers, big auld fat sausages [not nice and dainty like now] as a must if we could afford them. We would have a fierce feed on a Saturday evening when we came home. All the children and ourselves were full as anything as we would have a big fry and have eaten all around us.

We used to be able to kill a beast back in those days too. A small little heifer. We would get it done up in the butchers. You would have meat for the whole year then and be so grateful for it. You wouldn't be putting down big pots of it and it not be eaten not like now. Then they brought it that you couldn't kill the beast so that was the end of that.

Holts Hardware was another shop I remember very well in Edenderry. We might need pieces for the bike, maybe a bicycle pump and they always took care of us.

Michael Ward was the solicitor in the town at that time. There was a man's barber in that direction as well. Bob would get his hair cut while I'd sit in the van and wait. I'd have all my money spent [as she laughs].
I mustn't forget Margaret Daly's too, the drapery. It was at the very corner. She always had very good clothes and not too dear. You would pay them off weekly as you called in every week. Maybe five shillings off at a time . We wouldn't bring them until they were paid for. And then you would step out in all your style. Maybe for a first communion or something. Edenderry was a great town with great people and still is. You would never be short of anything. And we were always grateful for all the people we use to meet in there too.

What advice would you give people nowadays regarding money?

I think we probably get money a bit too easy nowadays. And spend it too foolishly. I don't know do we think enough before we spend it. Too much money would destroy any young family if they don't mind themselves. And their marriages as well. And you often see that happening nowadays which is an awful pity.

If we got a half a crown when I was young, we would have it for so long just looking at it and we would get hard to spend it. And it's very much not like that nowadays. Now I'm not saying it's bad so to speak, but I just think we could think about the value of money a bit more. The majority of people were struggling back in my younger days. A good lot would be waiting for the fair in Kinnegad to sell a couple of cattle. It would happen every couple of months or even every three months. Rent and rates on your house would also be a big worry. Jack Keegan would come collect your rates. And then you would post your rent. Rates were maybe 15 or 16 pounds every three months or less for the county council. That's Sally McCabe father. He went around to all the houses in the area. You would hear him coming whistling. Once he went, you would put by money every week for his next visit. You dare not touch that.

We really had very little when we were growing up. The pension was only five shillings. One shilling for bread, one shilling for milk and sure you had little left then. God things have changed so much haven't they Louise?

They have Granny. You have seen it come full circle that is for sure.
If you have money nowadays Louise, you can have anything you want. That's where it's gone wrong in my thinking. With money you can buy a car, a house, anything you want. The world is your oyster. You can even hire a man or a woman for the night [as she laughs].

What advice would you give people nowadays regarding religion/faith?
It is important to have a faith. My faith is very important to me. If I could go to mass now, I'd be there only for this old virus. I love seeing families going out together and going to mass. You always feel better after going to mass. There is something about it. When you see the church you will feel better. The priest have to work so hard, and we don't know half of the work that goes on behind the scenes. I love mass as well for the sense of community it brings. It's nearly the only place now where you would meet anyone out and about. It's a great opportunity to see your neighbours and your friends.

Do you love your faith Granny?
Thank God I have a faith. I'm not over religious. I hope my children and grandchildren might follow my faith in any little way. I don't think there

will be any priest or nuns in my family [as she laughs]. It's good to have a faith because it helps keep us all on the right track. It's good to know you can have a chat and share your problems with God above at any time. That's the great thing about God and all our saints, angels and family in Heaven, they are always listening, night noon and morning. God is overflowing with all I'm telling him and all I'm asking him every day. He never refused me yet. I don't mind not getting an answer immediately because I'll have asked him a few extra ones by the time he gets around to me. Just thinking here to myself, maybe if people had a little more interest in God, maybe they wouldn't do as many bad things. They wouldn't be going out to take people's lives even some of their own families. I try best as I can to pray for those who do bad things. And God love their families, and anyone hurt by another person. Sure, it's so sad isn't it. So many people fighting for their lives with cancer, strokes and in hospitals and then there are others killing people. It breaks my heart.

Why do people do bad things?

I don't know. I just wonder how their conscience does not get to them? As I look around our country and the world, I see so many murders happening. I feel sorry for their parents and families trying to fix them up again or how they handle it. All I can do is pray for everyone.

Why do bad things happen to good people?

I'm sorry I really can't give a straight answer to that Louise. I often think of it myself when I see good people and bad things happening them. Maybe God might repay them in a different way. I know many good people who help and do charity. And then there are bad people doing bad for no reason. It makes no sense. And now I'm sitting here so much thinking to myself, I work often on my mind to find the answer. I wish I could.

What advice do you have if you end up on your own? You were left as a widow in 1989, how did you cope with that?

Well, I never regretted living on my own. I always had plenty of little and big jobs to do. I knitted and crocheted. I never went out much at night at all. I always found something to be doing. I was never depressed about it or sad. I spent a lot of time doing up the house. There was a lot to do.

And I'm a big believer to keep busy is the key. If you have a little garden, try and plant something. Cleaning up the walls inside or doing anything to keep you busy is my advice.

You've lived here on your own for a lifetime Granny, did you ever get afraid at night?

Once I know the front door is locked at night, I would never be worried. I'd be afraid if anyone knocked very hard on the door now. Once you don't have a big open chimney you are lucky because you don't hear much outside and that has been my blessing. This is a wonderful house to block out the noises outside. Sure, you wouldn't hear a thing in here thank God. This is a lovely house and I count myself so lucky it's been my home for so long.

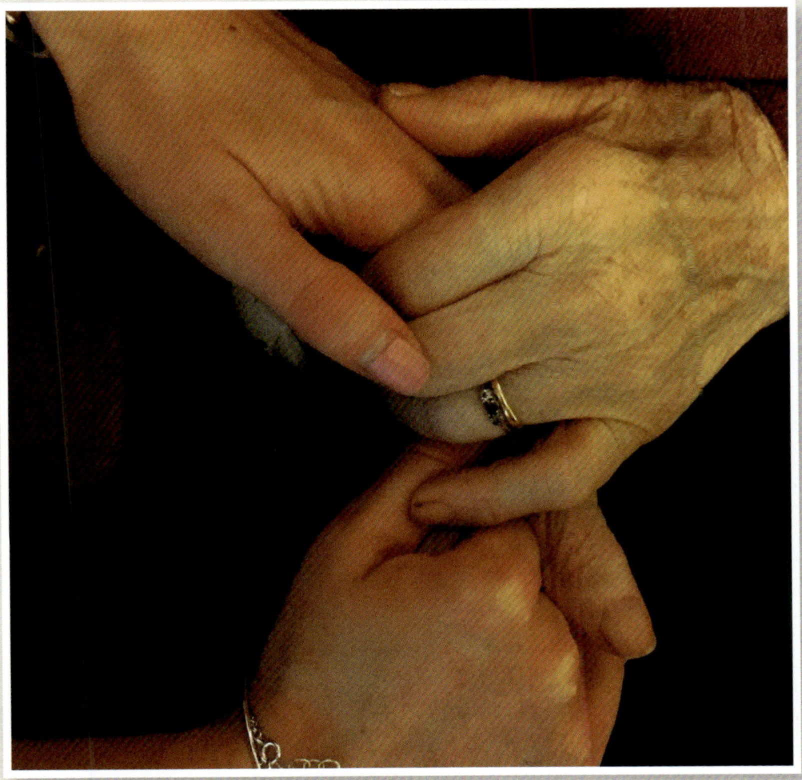

I'll never not miss those cute little hands of yours Gran. Thank God for photos.

Life can be tough can't it Gran, especially if someone suffers a stroke or something like that?

I don't like to see anyone suffer. Even to break a limb, you can repair it. But for someone to suffer a stroke Louise, it's awful hard altogether. I don't like to see that. I just pray for them. God love them all. And also, anyone suffering from dementia or Alzheimer's, it's just terrible. Often, it's those looking on that suffer the most in these stories, the person themselves don't know and I can't even imagine the families pain. I give you my prayers if you are reading this and need some strength if you are in this situation. The only part I can relate to is my daughter Margaret, one of the twins in Kerry, suffered that awful disease Motor Neurone. Her family and friends were so good to her down there and we use to travel down as much as we could to see her. It was heart breaking as a mother to watch her lose all her physical power and then for her to decline. I wouldn't wish it on anyone. The only thing I can say now is Margaret and her sister Anne are up in Heaven and I've no doubt they are having great laughs together. I'll meet them again one day and it will be great to see Margaret free of her disease when I do.

Gran's beautiful cat Tom

Do you like cats or dogs?

Often old women like me like to have a cat or dog close by. Hugging them and talking to them. But I'm not one for that. I like the cat, but I like where he is. Out in the yard! He's a very obedient cat because he just does his own thing. He's a bit like me [as she laughs to herself]. I do love your dog, Louise. Daisy is a lovely dog. She's very good, isn't she? I couldn't believe how quiet she is and yet so friendly. Just like me, right? [She laughs again]

I took this photo in May 2020 when we experienced that amazing summer weather. Me and Gran loved spending time in her beautiful garden and of course there wasn't a day when Gran didn't look pretty.

Gran loved baking and there was nothing quite like bread made by her beautiful hands.

CHAPTER NINE
ONE WORD OR THREE TO DESCRIBE . . .

Myself and Granny having a giggle on her beautiful couch with her famous crochet blanket in the background.

I decided to ask Gran to give one-word responses on different topics I would mention. She started off good but her natural chatty self-started to bypass the rules of one word answers and gave me quite full length responses and I couldn't but leave them in. Now you know where I get all my words from. Granny, I get my chatty skills from you and I wouldn't change it for the world. Further down the conversation I started to flesh out different topics and she really enjoyed this line of questions too as you will see as you read on.

The Irish Weather: Unpredictable

The Pope: A normal kind man. I never met him but only through talk. But he seems to be a very nice gentleman. And maybe if I live long enough, I might have the pleasure of meeting him.

What kind of person is God? He's kind.

Your Carers: The definition of kindness. They are all very kind to me. And I hope I return the good kindness to them too. They always come in smiling and I'm so grateful to them. They are such good friends to me, and I'd be lost without them. I'm very lucky.

Clonard: Home. I made it my home when I married Bob and it's been my home for a lifetime now. There are so many kind people in Clonard, and I hope I'm as kind to them. I never even thought I was known at all, but I seem to be a bit now.

Your Faith: Strong. I like my faith. I like to be a good catholic if I can at all.

What happens after someone passes on?
I do be here sitting and do be thinking what Heaven and hell is like. Hell is gone now thank God. That bucket there could be hell if you lit it. Imagine being thrown into that. Heaven is a magical place but it's a pity nobody can come back and tell us.

What's heaven like?
If we don't get fed will we die from hunger up there [laughing loads].

Your Body: I suppose we could say my body was very healthy. I had trouble with my eyes when I was young. Got them looked after and they are great now. I just keep an eye on them [as she laughs]. I never had a broken bone until I was one hundred and five. God hardly let me suffer at all with a broken hip. He spared me and he was so kind to me. He said I suffered enough during my life keeping childer under control that he let me through that moment.

Your Mind: Thank God he gave me a very clear mind. I never sit down all day worrying. See the thing about worrying is that it's neither good for who you are worrying for or good for yourself. They will all figure it out for themselves and ourselves. We should all leave it to God.

Your Heart: I've a strong heart. I never had any trouble with it. It got broke a few times. It got mended over time. I still miss all my family and friends who are in heaven but I'm lucky I have a good heart.

Ireland: I love Ireland and I'm a very proud Irish woman. We're a great little country. The people are the salt of the earth.

Myself and Gran dressed up in our Irish gear to celebrate our love of our little country! We had such a laugh as you can see.

Older People: I think the older people are often forgotten in this country. Things are moving very fast now with technology. If you don't have someone to show you how to use it or enjoy it, like I have you Louise, you would be left behind. I think also more help should be put in place for people to live and die in their own homes if that is their wish. I think I've kept so good because I'm at home. Home is where the heart is, and nobody should be unnecessarily taken from their home if they don't want to. If anything, I could be an example of the good life one can have if let live at home until I die please god. I've always wanted to die in my own home and in my own bed if I'm really lucky, so hopefully, God can help me with that. But for now, I won't worry about it, I'll just enjoy each day I wake up and I'm well.

What's your favourite county Gran? Oh, county Meath of course. Born and bred a Meath woman I am, and you couldn't get a better county. Home is home.

Gran was thrilled to be part of the celebrations in Clonard GAA when the ladies silverware came to visit the village.

What's your favourite flower?

Begonias would be my favourite. They are beautiful. They are red and yellow. They used to be that colour anyways, but they could be any colour nowadays with everything they can do.

What's your favourite colour?

Well, black is a very reliable colour because it looks nice on you no matter who you are. But really, I'm a woman of the colours when it comes to clothes so I'd get hard to pick. I like red. Not deep red. Bright cherry red is lovely. But then I like pink and green too, oh and yellow. Actually, now that I think of it I like all colours. I love a bright baby blue too like the virgin mother. I have a cardigan that colour, and I love it. When I think about it, I love bright colours and all types of them so I probably don't have a favourite because they are all my favourite.

What would be your three favourite eating houses?

Well, I could pick loads of them but I'll pick three. These eating houses all know me well. I love The Monastery Inn, Clonard, County Meath. That's here in the village. We are so lucky to have such a lovely restaurant in our little village and sure everyone loves it. Oh, I love Mother Hubbard's in Moyvalley in County Kildare. That's just down the road from Clonard. A very popular place too. It's closed now because of that old virus but I'm hoping it opens back up because the staff are so lovely, and they treat me as Granny. And sure I can't forget the good old Harry's of Kinnegad in County Westmeath. Everyone across the country knows Harry's. It's nearly been there as long as myself. And I'll have to mention Scanlon's as well in Kinnegad and while I'm here not forgetting 'The Hamlet Court Hotel' in Johnstownbridge where I had my 100th birthday. Let's just say we had a great time there and the O'Neill's always look after me so well. There are so many people I could mention but I hope ye all know how much I think of ye all.

Myself and Granny were always the best of friends.
This is us together at her 100th Birthday party.

What would be your three favourite hymns or songs Gran?

Oh Louise, now that's a hard one. Sure we love listening to so many new ones these days, but I guess in life, sometimes the old ones really are the best. I love 'Hail Queen of Heaven' by that lovely gentleman we love, James Kilbane is his name, and he also sings 'Bring Flowers of the Rarest' beautifully. And the last hymn I'll pick is the lovely Daniel O'Donnell singing 'Lady of Knock'. We're not Ireland's best singers sure we're not Louise[!], but we definitely love singing them together that's for sure. I've had so much joy with you listening to all sorts of songs. You can do so much on that phone of yours, it's magic nearly.

I used to try and surprise Gran with little treats during the intense lockdowns. Gran loved the goodies I ordered for us from Patisserie 2210 in Mullingar.

What's your favourite sweets?

Jelly babies or jellies. I like the Athlone sweets ones, the big juicy jellies or just the ordinary Jelly Babies. But you know me, I'd eat anything you give me [laughs to herself again].

Gran's house was dressed in colour for her 107th birthday.

What would be your favourite prayer Gran? I know this is a hard one for you to pick and we have tipped on this before.

You know how I love my prayers. I love them all and sure God is great for listening to me. They have been my saviour in getting older really. Because no matter how you are feeling or if your body is not able, you can always say a prayer for yourself or for someone else. They have kept me so well, especially my mind and my heart. My favourite prayer if I was to pick one would be the Hail Holy Queen. I'll say it now;

Hail Holy Queen, Mother of Mercy, Hail our Light,
Our sweetness and our hope.
To thy, we cry poor banished children of Eve,
To thy, we send up our sighs mourning's and weeping's in this valley of tears.
Turn then most gracious advocate your eyes of mercy towards us,

and after this our exile shown to us in the Blessed fruit of thy womb Jesus.
Oh Clement, Oh Loving, Oh Sweet Virgin Mary,
Pray for us oh Holy Mother of God, that we may be made worthy of the promises of Christ.
God bless us all and spare us our health.

Sure how would you not like that prayer, it covers everything. And I love when we say it together Louise. I think God must be very happy with the two of us. I've said that now for anyone reading our book. Imagine. A book about my life. I never thought I'd hear that being said. Sure I'm laughing here now thinking about it. You're very good at the typing there Louise. So fast.

Who's your favourite celebrity?
I don't like to make a real favourite as you know Louise. It's a selfish thing to have a real favourite. I can't think of anyone really that sticks out in my mind. I do love Catherine Leydon, the baking lady now that I think about it. She was all our favourites in the baking department down through the years and still is, so I'll pick Catherine, our Odlum's woman.

Who's your favourite singer?
Myself [Laughing heartily to herself]. That's a good one, isn't it?

You're very funny Granny. You are a wonderful singer. You're my favourite singer. But I was wondering was there anyone else you enjoyed singing?
Oh, I thought for a second you were asking me now, what is my favourite dinner? [and she laughs to herself]. You know how I love my food. It's always on my mind. Oh, my favourite singer is Daniel O'Donnell. He was very good to me. Himself and his lovely wife Majella rang us. Remember Louise when he rang. Wasn't that great? And so kind of him to do so. I also love hymns by everyone and anyone. There was a hymn on Radio Maria, and I loved it. It was something about feet. I said I must remember that, but I couldn't remember it. They might play it again tomorrow.

You love listening to the radio Granny? What would be your favourite radio station?
Radio Maria is my favourite because I'm never lonely when it's on. I can say my prayers, lots of chats and lots of hymns. It's brilliant. I always love

RTE Radio One. I've listened to it all my life. This station has all the latest and I love it. It's been a wonderful find during these lockdowns. I was awful lonely, but Radio Maria gave me great company. Louise, you were great to find it for me and sure we're tuned into it from morning until night. I was even on it with Louise saying the rosary. I think I did a great job of it. I hope they liked me on there. I think they did.

Two ladies who not only love their scarves but love to enjoy life to the full.

Had women a hard time when you were younger?
The men were always the bosses. Most men handled the money. They were the head of the house. Some men were bossier than others. Bob was very good to me though. He would give it to me no bother. Money was very scarce back then. Or very secretly handled could I say maybe would be a better turn of phrase. You wouldn't be running out saying you had so much money. If people thought you had it, they would try

and become friendly with you. Or if you got a lot of jobs done, then they would overcharge you. We were always saving, even if we didn't know what we were saving for. School books and copies all were pricey back then. Nowadays there are a lot more grants and supports and that's a good thing. Everything has become cheaper all round. Sure now everyone wants to shout about all the money they have instead of keeping it quiet. I'm still a big believer that a quiet word about anything you have, will serve you better in the long run. I'm not a fan of people bragging. It's not a nice trait.

Women were such all-rounders back then. Even down to being good knitters and sewers, sure they would be doing jobs for other families as well as their own. If they were dressmakers, they would make shirts for the men. Back then women were skilled in ways we no longer need to be nowadays. It's much less stressful thank God and things have got a lot easier all round. It was very hard work back in the day to be a woman.

How are women treated nowadays?
They have a great time now. They have an easier time I would say just based on my own experience because there are plenty of good jobs with plenty of good pay. But compared to the old days, we have come a long way. Now I'm not saying women have it easy, no way am I saying that. But thank God we finally got our foot in, and we now get the respect we deserve and we're not slaves to a million jobs. Not like the old days. It really was such hard work.

Any advice on how young people could learn about the world Granny?
Long ago, youngsters would be out digging ground. Digging plots. You wouldn't see that nowadays and that's probably not great. It would be good for young people to plant a few vegetables, weed a few plots, see how it's done and see the rewards for their work. There is nothing better than learning through a process and then reaping the reward of learning something practical like a plot of vegetables. I'm telling you the weeding alone would teach you a lot about life. There is nothing as tedious as weeding and it would sure carve out a character in someone not to give up. One minute you think you have all the weeds, the next minute they are all back again. I think these sorts of things really help build resilience in people. And also, you learn where everything, particularly food comes from and sure everyone should know that. It's good for

young people to see the process and be part of it. We won't always be here for them so it's important we teach them skills in case there was a food shortage or crisis of any kind. It's not fair not to give them some real-life practical skills. Not everything can be done on a computer. I just think it's important to have a balance.

I was so thrilled I organised a mass for Gran's 106th Birthday as we all enjoyed it immensely and it was all before Covid came knocking.

Have you always liked to be dressed well?

I always had my good clothes. My mam was very good at dressing well now that I think about her. She always looked beautiful as I was growing up as a child. Skirts and blouses were the fashion back in the day of course. The first that wore the trousers was nearly put out of the parish. Isn't it some change nowadays when you think about it? It's great though. They were silly rules thinking back. Thank God now us women can wear what we like. Let everyone have their own opinion that's what I think. I love my skirt for good occasions nowadays and then I keep my trousers for around the house. It's so lovely that we now have so much choice.

Oh, and I also love my gloves. Loads of the lovely Facebook family have sent me presents of gloves of all colours and types. I have choices now when it comes to my gloves. It's unbelievable the generosity shown to me and some of them I haven't even met, would you believe that Louise?

I would Granny. Sure, they love you like I love you. We have done so many videos with the Facebook family, we love them all. And I know they enjoy our fun and messing together. We do love a good laugh that is for sure.

Granny was always up for fun and laughter and she particularly loved the camera filters.

What do you think about stress?

Oh let it off. Don't let it get you down. But I feel bad for anyone who owes a lot of money. Imagine someone coming to the door and you not having money to meet the payment. But what I try to say if you're stressed is to say a little prayer and try not worry about it. People worry a lot nowadays and it's not good for their health or their heads. I guess with the world as it is it's hard not to worry but I put all my faith in God that he will mind us all and he hasn't let me down yet. Try not to worry. It usually never happens whatever we are imagining. Make yourself a cup of tea and get something nice to eat and then you might forget about your troubles. If you are still worried, pick up the phone and call a friend. I find that is a great resolution for worry, a good friend can lighten your stress. And if you can have a cup of tea with them too, well then you are on a winner.

You're rubbing your hands together there Granny?

I was asking St. Brigid to sort out my hands. I do have the odd pain, but she will have to go off with herself if she doesn't help me out [laughing to herself looking up at the four St. Brigid's crosses around her room]. I'm only messing really because I love St. Brigid. She's very special. You like her too don't you Louise? Sure I love all the saints. I asked St. Anthony for lots of things, and he never fails me either. I'm well able to get around thank God. I love my home. Lord when I look up to my two holy pictures above my bed, I say thank God and I thank God again in my prayers. I have my picture of St. Teresa, the little flower and then our lady and her baby in the other picture. And of course, then I have my St. Brigid's crosses both sides of me in my room and my little cross I was given as a gift. When I think of our lady and she going to the temple and getting the little lord out on her knee. I love my two pictures. They mean everything to me. Every time I look up, I say to myself I'm so lucky to be in my home. Once I see them, I know I'm safe, happy and loved. I'm as happy as Larry once I see my own auld house and that I can get in and out. And once I have my family and friends coming in sure I couldn't be happier. I love them all. I hope they know that. I think they do.

Your thoughts on our native language? Should we speak it more?

I heard a lot of women the other day talking Irish on the radio. I said to myself it's a pity we don't hear more Irish used in our everyday life. Every other country has their own language. I think I suppose the English coming over here took it off us really, we can't deny that. We probably should have held onto it tighter. But I guess it better to be able to speak English now as so many countries like coming here because we speak English. So, there's two sides to every story isn't there? I have to say all my idle time goes into praying and I can even say a few of my prayers in Irish. I'm a proud Irish woman myself and I love our little country. I say little Hail Mary's for anyone who needs them all the time. I have my rosary beads on my arm the whole time. And of course, I'll bless myself in Irish too. I don't think I'm keeping the language alive but it's nice to say a little prayer in Irish.

Who have you in your family?

I have one Son Finian who is in London. I have Kathleen, Mary, and Olive at home here which is very convenient too. They have always been very good to me, and I am grateful to all of them for everything they have done for me over the years. I had twins but I lost them when they were about 42 or 43. One with Motor Neurone and the other her sister died with lonesomeness for her. But that's my whole life but thank God I'm fresh and hardy thank God.

I'm getting wonderful care from my children, my grandchildren and the carers coming in every day and Louise living with me, so I don't have much to be complaining about. Since the pandemic hit, I just have my few special people in and my carers. I have my carers who are so kind to me, and I love to hear them coming in. I love to say hello to them and talk to them and I love to tell them how much I appreciate them and thanks to be God I'm so well looked after. God bless them all.

Do you miss all your visitors?

Oh god I miss them all so much. Hopefully it won't be too long before we are back together chatting in the kitchen and drinking tea.

What age do you feel?

I feel about sixty. I don't even know how I got to one hundred. And now look at me getting to one hundred and seven. We will have another party for one hundred and eight. I'm looking forward to that now. I love my birthday. It's a great get together normally. I know with this old virus it's not the same but maybe it will be gone for my 108th birthday. I hope so because it would be lovely to see all my friends, my grandchildren, my great grandchildren, my great-great grandchildren, my nephews and nieces, my cousins and not forgetting all my neighbours and my family. That's all that matters to me. And all the lovely people who I haven't got to meet yet because of Covid. I've made so many friends from Facebook with you Louise. They are so kind to me always sending me messages. And not to mention parcels, cards, rosary beads, gloves scarves and chocolates and the list goes on and on and on.

What advice would you give to keep hopeful in this world?
Try and say a few prayers and ask your favourite saint to help you. Get up and do a few jobs and take your mind off the worry. I like to pray when I sit down. I don't say a special one just for one person, I join a few together sometimes

So Gran, would you believe that's all my questions. You have been absolutely wonderful and I can't believe I'm going to say this, but I'm so thankful for the lockdown's for this very special moment. I would never have got the time to have interviewed you so much and had so much fun with you only for all this quiet time. It is true what they say, that sometimes good things can come out of bad times and this is very true. Thanks so much Granny for all your answers and for allowing me to write and record all our interviews for the book. How do you feel?
Sure I couldn't' be happier Louise. I am in my own home and sure aren't we making the best of this time together. We could sit here and winge and cry all day if we wanted but instead we are having a great time. And sure don't mention the amount of tea we are drinking, the fun we are having and all the new friends I am making and I'm not even leaving my armchair. Where would you get it? I loved doing the baking with you and I love the masses and everything we get up to. There are too many good memories to mention. I wouldn't be here without you Louise and I hope you know how important you are to me. Sure we are best friends. I've been so lucky to have such a wonderful family all my life and great friends and neighbours who have all taken care of me. I hope they know how grateful I am to them all. This is why I say my prayers Louise, to say thanks to God for minding me so well and for giving me such wonderful people around me. I don't know when he will come to take me but one thing I know is I've had a wonderful time here and I have been blessed with such a loving family, lovely carers and wonderful friends. I hope when my time comes to leave, people might say 'oh that Nancy one, she

lived a great life, ate lots, laughed lots and loved lots too.' That sounds like I did it right doesn't it Louise?

It does Granny. You definitely lived a wonderful life and we are all so grateful that we got to be a part of it.

Righteo you must have my life all written down now. I don't know will anyone even want to read it. But it's good we did this Louise. You know what I'm going to say now don't you?

I've a feeling I do Granny . . .

It must be time for tea [as she lays back in her seat and laughs heartily]

It sure is Gran. It's time for tea and lots of it.

Gran's beautiful smile was known all over the world along with her love for a cup of tea in her favourite cup.

CHAPTER TEN

THE DEPARTING OF GRANNY NANCY

Granny's one wish in her whole life was to die in her own bed in her own home. She mentioned it quite a few times in this book. One would think and know well, that in life, for the majority of us, we don't too often get what we want. Instead, most things seem to go against us, but in this story, I do indeed have a happy and joyful ending to it. Since this part is now over to me, it gives me great peace to share with you that Granny did indeed leave this world for the next in her own bed in her own home on the 10th of September 2021 around 5.45am. Granny didn't know she was leaving and either did I. We had been up all night talking which is not at all unusual. Like us all, there were nights where Gran just couldn't sleep so on that Thursday night when I went into see how she was at 11.30pm. I could hear her mooching in her bed. Her words to me were "it's one of those nights Louise. I just can't seem to sleep."

We ended up staying up all night talking, praying and drinking tea. It was not something I was anyway unsettled about and just thought it was another 'one of those nights'. But come the morning breaking and the birds singing, and a new day upon us, within a breath and whilst holding my hand, Gran slipped away. There was no drama. No illness. No pain. No suffering. Instead, God must have asked her, do you want to leave now Nancy, and she must have said "Yes God I'm ready to meet all my family and friends in Heaven now. My time here is over and my work here is done." And in that instant, she let go of my hand and went to meet all our loved ones up above the big blue sky and I've no doubt she now sits somewhere between the sun and the moon and close to a rainbow.

There is no way I can describe how much I miss her. She became my full focus and my life. In many ways she was my little baby and yet she was a 107-year-old lady who offered so much fun and wisdom in equal measure. As they say, they don't make them like this anymore. I was very lucky and blessed by covid landing really. I know there aren't too many that would feel like that, but the pandemic gave me the gift of intense and intimate time with Granny. If not for the lockdowns, I would never have got to spend such a special time with her and this book would just be a far-off idea. It would not have become a reality. And for that alone, I will always be so grateful.

There is no doubt, our time together was very special, and I feel every fibre of her in my heart, mind and soul ever since she departed. Gran's family and friends miss her dearly, and I know that is a common thread across us all. And wonderfully and miraculously it's not sadness, instead it's appreciation and an awareness of luck. Luck that we got to love and know this lady. A sense of fortune that we spent time with a real-life miracle and a living saint. I will forever miss you Granny but more importantly I will forever love you and hold you in my heart. I was blessed with a moment in my life where I got to hold your hand every day and I will always be forever grateful for that blessing. I will live my life with you by my side and I know you have us all covered in prayers and miracles up there in Heaven. I know you have made so many new friends already and all your old pals and family must have been over the moon to see you walking through the gates. Tell St. Anthony, Mary, Joseph, Jesus, St. Theresa and all the gang I say hello. I'm sure you have them all baking white soda breads and no doubt watching Facebook live. All my love my dearest friend and grandmother

When you see me looking up, know that I'm looking to you. Look forward to us reuniting when my time comes but until then, I'll try do you proud down here.
Lou x

CHAPTER ELEVEN
A POEM ABOUT NANCY AND A LETTER OF HOPE, LIGHT & LOVE

NANCY STEWART - 100 YEARS YOUNG

By Louise Coghlan

(October 2013)

In 1913, a lady was born,
100 years later, it's her birthday morn.
Could you believe it, it's not often true,
If you ask her, the century, it flew.

This birthday is special, this lady is real,
Her mind, body . . . able . . . her smile the genuine deal.
Her life it has been long, yet fast it has gone,
She never sits down, unless Fair City is on.

Her name is Nancy Stewart and to lots, she is theirs,
We all want a piece of her, her love is in layers.
We are young, we are old,
We are family, friends to hold,
She is fab, she is kind.
She is ours, a gem to find.

Life can be short, life can be long,
But with Nancy around, life is a song.
She loves so many parts, of the world as it sits,
She is like to life, a part that just fits.

Her baking, her flowers, her garden, her patch,
Her skills are just endless, that no one could match.
She sings as she knits, she smiles as she cooks,
You would never believe her age, with her beauty, her looks.

It is on this very day, we celebrate this woman,
Her attitude, her passion, she's our special someone,
How lucky we are, to have such a friend,
They say in one's life, an angel on earth God will send,
It is Nancy that lights up our world's every day,
To each of us, always, a kind words she does say.

As you celebrate your 100 years with us, we smile to each other,
Knowing there is no one like you, you're like Cinderella's Godmother.
We just want you to know, how much we do love you,
Gran, you're magic, amazing and inspiring too.

If ever I feel like the world is a hard place, I think of your smile,
Your warm loving grace.
You pick me up when I need it most,
You can fix it with a cup of tea and your famous toast.

If this world gives me nothing, but your happy smile,
I know I've been blessed by an absolute mile,
As long as your kettle is boiling, and the lights they are on,
We owe you so much, our friendship the happiest song.

And in my last lines, there's not much to say,
Only you are one of life's miracles in your very special way.
Thank you so much for all that you do,
100 years for us it just flew,
Your glowing smile you always have on,
Bring on the next party where you turn a hundred and one!

The three amigos and the three generations of women who were always smiling together .

That time we were on Channel 4 with the very lovely Steph on Steph's Lunch. Granny was as cool as a cucumber as we broadcasted live via zoom for the whole show.

'A LETTER OF HOPE' - (2020)

To the People of Ireland and the World,

My name is Nancy Stewart, and I was born on the 16th of October 1913. This weekend I turn 107 years of age. Imagining turning 107 in a world pandemic. This definitely is something very unusual even for me and all I have been through. I live in Clonard in County Meath and have lived in my home for over 83 years. I lost my husband Bob, in a car crash in 1989 and lost my twin daughters Margaret in 2007 to motor neurone and Anne in 2010 to utter heartbreak of losing her sister. I've lost all my friends throughout the years which comes with living so long on this earth. I'm very lucky to still have three daughters Kathleen, Mary and Olive and one son Finian and I have 84 grandchildren, great grandchildren and great great grandchildren. I have faced many heart-breaking moments and also have seen many hard times in our country witnessing world wars, division in our people and numerous sad times for our nation.

I write to you today to send you my love and to offer you my prayers. We are in a very difficult time at the moment in our country, in our lives and in our world. But I reach out to you in this letter to offer you hope, faith and belief that everything will be okay in the end. We are in another stage of this battle against the virus, but we will get through this. Like everything I've been through since the day I was born in 1913, no matter how bad things have got, I'm the living proof that we can survive and in years to come, this will just be a distant memory.

I have a great faith and it has helped me keep positive throughout the struggles I've met. I thank you for keeping your faith and for keeping your resilience strong, through this hard time. Sadly, for the moment, we can no longer stretch out to a friend and embrace them nor can we call to each other's houses.

But I'm here to share my story. I have been in lockdown in my house since March, alongside my granddaughter Louise and even though it has been a tough time, we have got through it together. We drink tea. We say prayers. We bake. We laugh. We make phone calls. I can even video call lots of my family and friends and am making new friends every day that God gives me on this earth.

And that's a very important thing to say. If you are feeling low, make sure to try call someone or even go for a walk. I also ask God to help me if I'm feeling low. This is a hard time for everyone but please make sure you keep yourself well and wear your mask. If you keep healthy, your mind will stay healthy too. Keep talking to one another. All my life I have always believed in chatting and drinking tea and saying a prayer or a decade of the rosary and it has got me through. This is our moment to keep our faith and to keep believing that everything will turn out okay. We must try and make sure we leave nobody behind and also that we don't lose sight of each other. This is a moment for humanity to step forward to take care of the other. We must mind ourselves, but we must also mind all those around us. Look up and smile even if you have your mask on. Your eyes will smile and that might be all someone needs to keep going. No good deed ever goes unnoticed so try your best to keep being good. We are not here to live for ourselves but to live for each other.

I can't believe I've made it to this age; I only feel like I'm fifty but now that I'm here, all I can say is please God I'll be here for my next birthday. We must always look forward. I can't believe I'm the oldest person in Ireland living in my own home, I don't feel that old. When God wants me, he will come take me but for now I will keep enjoying my life, I'll keep loving my family and I'll keep saying my prayers day by day . . . oh and not to forget eating lots of good wholesome food is my tip. Good food and lots of tea is my secret to a long life as well as keeping positive as best we can. We must always look forward and hope for the best.

Thank you for thinking of me in your prayers and your thoughts and I promise I will think of you in my many rosaries I say every day. Thank you so much for reading my letter also and I hope I have, in even a little way, helped you feel less alone in this moment. There is always hope and once we keep talking to one another, no day will seem empty, and we can get through this together. It only takes a small candle to take away the dark and in each of us, we can be that light in the world.

This hard time will indeed pass like all the rest and all that matters is that we helped each other through.

Many blessings and much love,
Granny Nancy Stewart and Lou Coghlan x [October 2020]

The younger versions of Granny and myself alongside the older, wiser and funnier version of ourselves.

'A LETTER OF LIGHT' - (2020)

To all the people of Ireland and across our lovely world

My name is Louise Coghlan and I'm 37 years of age and beside me is Granny Nancy Stewart and she's 107 years of age and we live together in Clonard, County Meath.

We write to you today to offer you our light in a time where the world is still making its way through what has been a very hard year for us all. Yes, we are now in the final month of 2020 and we are so proud of each and every one of ye for making it this far. This has not been an easy journey. This has not been anything of what we expected for 2020 and even though we have made it to the end of this year, many have not. Many of our countrywomen and men have left this world for the next not just through Covid19 taking them but through lots of different illnesses and accidents taking them away from their families forever. Lots of our friends have been hurt terribly by 2020 and lots of hearts are feeling broken and lost at this moment in time. Lots of our neighbours, companions and loved ones are feeling weighed down by the darkness of this year and are struggling to find a light to guide them beyond this moment. Many awake every morning unsure of how they will survive the day ahead. This letter is for YOU! We know, there is nothing as heavy as a broken heart, a broken mind or a worried soul. Today, we write these words to stretch out our hands to you and offer our strength to help you keep going. To help you feel not so alone at this heart-broken time. We are here for you, and we promise everything will be okay in the end.

In life, we never know what's around the corner for any of us and we think it's fair to say that 2020 could be defined by that statement alone. If we are to learn anything this year, we think it's that. We really have very little control on what life is going to throw at us. No matter who we are, no matter where we work or if we are without work, no matter how much money is in our bank account or how little, no matter the size of our home or if we are homeless . . . life will deal you cards that you cannot control. Our fate is destined by something greater than us. But what we do have control on, is ourselves and our own individual efforts and reactions within this world. We can indeed control how we treat each other, how we speak to each other, how we help each other, how we make each other feel and most importantly how we cope when bad things happen. These we feel are the most important strokes of wisdom we as humans need to focus on as 2020 closes. There are people reading this that need us to help them see the step ahead as they are lost in their grief, their heartbreak or are just feeling low at this time. Grief is a guarantee for us all. Once we love another human, grief will one day come knocking on our heart. We must be actively showing kindness to each other when we can because one day it will be us with our heads bowed down and our hearts broken. At this moment in time, there are many people lost in their sadness of a cross that bears heavy on their daily lives. It's over to us to hold a light out from our hearts to help guide them from their darkness. This must be the focus for 2021 for each of us as individuals but also as a nation and as a world. We must learn from what 2020 has being trying to teach us. We must not step into a new year and not learn that the most important part of being a human is to the gift and the superpower of shining a light for someone who is lost in the darkness. And at any moment, we might be the ones needing that light shone. Life is as fragile as a dream.

Granny and I decided to write this letter to offer our light as we face into the end of 2020. This time of year is usually associated with joy and fun, laughter and get together but for this year, it will different. It will be strained in many ways for many people. This can be a time of intense loneliness and I think for us all we have been reminded of the fragility of life and the fragility of our loved ones in this year more than any.

Both myself and gran have gone through our own heavy times in our own individual ways and understand how at this time of the year, your heart can feel extra broken and extra lonely. I lost my dad to rapid lung cancer six years ago and I was tortured for a long time in seeing him die in such pain and suffering and to leave within weeks of finding out his diagnosis, and my gran lost her husband in a car accident in 1989 while driving into mass. She never got to say goodbye to her dearly beloved soulmate and when she regained consciousness a week after the accident, her husband wasn't just gone but his funeral was over. Loneliness and grief are two of the heaviest crosses you will ever carry in your life and if you are feeling the weight of these struggles as you read this letter, we want to offer you our strength, our resilience and our promise that you will come through this very hard time. We offer you our story and our light to help you feel less alone if you are traveling your own path of darkness as your read this.

Gran and I are carrying a lantern of light within our hearts for you, and we have been in your shoes, and we can help you see the next step by sending these words to you. We are the proof that when the world for you feels empty of hope, love and light, we in this letter give you ours. We promise you everything will be okay in the end, and you can come through this very tough time. We ask you to stretch out to someone if you are feeling very low and want to remind that you are loved more than you could ever imagine. You can come through this darkness and back out into the light. It won't be today. It might not be tomorrow, or the day after that but I promise you, until that day we will shine our lantern of ever flowing light over you. We also have you wrapped up in our daily prayers and will send you all our strength. One day when you feel a bit brighter, maybe you might pass the lantern of light back to us when we don't feel so good ourselves. The gift and magic of the light is that it moves between humans, and only can you give it away when you too have felt the magic of it.

Keep looking up. Keep going. Keep being you. We will always be here for you.

Your friends of Light and Love,

Granny Nancy and Lou x [December 2020]

'A LETTER OF LOVE' - (2021)

To the People of Ireland and all across the world and to all who are listening today

I hope this letter finds you well. It has been quite a time since we last wrote to you all. It's Granny Nancy and Lou here penning you a word or two. We write this letter together as we have become like synchronised swimmers at this stage, where one looks to the other and then we just go for it. It's always worth going for another splash as words are powerful when sent from the heart of humans who care for each other and for the intention to help another human who might just be struggling.

As many of you know, my name is Granny Nancy and I'm nearly 108 years of age. My birthday is on the 16th of October of this year and it's hard to believe another year has passed. Life has been very unusual in the last 16 months or so, but we have survived, and we have coped. And that is the main thing I am here to remind you. In the letters I last wrote to you, I shared [that this pandemic will too pass] and at this moment in time, we are in the chapter that is 'passing', while not yet passed. In life we will learn, as I have on so many occasions, that resilience and patience are vital to see your way through a troublesome passage. In my lifetime, I have been through more tough times that I wish to recall but even though the ache is in my memory of the pains and struggles, I choose to focus on the good, the positive, the other side of the story. The part where I survived. And here I am today to remind you, that you too, will survive this chapter. Whether the weight of the complicated arms of covid are wearing you down or if you are struggling with life rocking you about, I am the reminder, the beacon, the light, the truth and also the hope for you to know that you will survive, you will come through whatever is making your heart heavy and you will step beyond it and life will be good to you again. Whenever you struggle just think to yourself, if Granny Nancy can survive and come through wars, pandemics, times of poverty and strain as well as losing many members of my family and my friends, you can too. And that is why we are writing this letter to give you hope to keep going. Louise is here too and she will add her lamp of light and love to this letter as follows

Hello there everyone. My name is Lou and I live with Granny Nancy. I'm one of her granddaughters and I've been living and laughing with Granny Nancy for quite some time now. I'm so grateful for what God has given me. In losing my job when Covid arrived, I became an overnight cocooner with this wonderful lady. She really is a special human and even though I'm biased by relation, I promise you, she is the real-life miracle we all need in the world today. Often, I forget that gran is the age she is, because she is so youthful in her nature. Yes, her body has slowed down in recent months but her mind, her soul and her spirit are as strong and as bright as the sun on a summer's morning. Granny will turn 108 years old on October 16th of this year and is the oldest lady in Ireland and of course living in her own home. I just want to share briefly my experience of this magical woman. When I look at her, I see joy, I see pain, I see light, I see shade but what I see most is a human who has been through it all and still has a smile upon her face. Granny Nancy is a living saint and I hope someday she will be recognised for what she has brought to the table of life for her country and for the world in her 108 years. Through our Facebook page 'Living and Laughing with Lou' together we have created a portal to share gran's infectious gift of loving life and for me I got to share my love of her through it. we have tried to spread endless hope to as many as we can and I think we have achieved it.

Often in life, we can think the hand we are dealt is a bit raw, but within days of starting my long cocoon with Granny I realised for me, covid had redirected a miracle into my life. And not a passing miracle, no, instead I was going to live my life learning all about it and in no time at all, I was going to love it. That miracle was the cutest little woman in the world, and I was being gifted her in a world pandemic. What I've learned in this time is very simple. Granny has taught me that you can be happy with very little. We've had the absolute time of our life sitting by her Jubilee stove laughing, chatting, praying and drinking tea. We've made so many friends as we reached out through social media and especially through our Facebook page and we wouldn't change a second of it.

As we sit here together writing this letter granny and I just want to say two simple words to you, THANK YOU. Thank you to all who have helped us step through this pandemic. We were not sure would we reach it to birthday number 108 but it's looking like the power of love can overcome anything. No matter the question Love is always the answer. Every day we get to spend together is a blessing and we just want to remind you that if Granny Nancy can survive two pandemics, no matter what comes knocking on your door, always remember a cup of tea, a prayer and a whole lot of love from someone who cares can carry you out of any storm. Roll on the birthday and don't forget, keep looking up. You're doing great and we're so very proud of you.

Much love and light from the two young messers on Facebook,

Granny Nancy and Lou x
**Read at the Funeral of Granny Nancy on September 10th 2021*

One of the many signs Gran continues to send me from Heaven in keeping her promise that we made to each other to comfort whoever would be left behind.

CHAPTER TWELVE

A LETTER FROM LOU TO GRANNY IN HEAVEN

Hi Granny,

I never thought I'd be writing a letter to you like this but I felt this was the best way for me to speak to you as I know you are reading every word as I type it. I've tried to write this quite a few times [as you know]but my broken heart kept stopping me finishing it but I've got a feeling this time I'll be able to reach the end.

Well, I guess the first and most important question I need to ask you, was the one I would ask you every morning that we woke together and that is how are you? I hope you are doing well and that have settled nicely into Heaven at this stage. You have been living there for just over a year now and my heart tells me you are very happy. I know you miss all your family and friends down here a lot but with the magic of Heaven I know you are so very close to us all of the time. We miss you terribly, the world doesn't seem the same without you in it, but I know with time, we will adjust and even though you are physically not here, we can feel you in a million ways. I can feel you everywhere Gran and as I write this, I'm looking up to your beautiful holy pictures that you loved so much in your bedroom where we spent so much time together. When I finish this, I will say some prayers and think of you ever so fondly.

This is a very special letter this time as all the letters before we wrote together but now, I am on my own. That is something nobody can prepare you for. I know every so often during our cocooning period, it crossed my mind as I put my head down on my fold up bed in the kitchen not sharing that thought with anyone but myself. I used to cry myself to sleep thinking about the scary reality of what would I do if ever you left me. Who would I be without you? It was a really scary thought and often I would wake with tears in my eyes where I would have even dreamed about it too. I would jump up and look to see that you were in your bed. And there you were, fast asleep and speedily I'd hop back into my bed with a big sigh of relief that it was just a nightmare. When it comes to grief, I had already experienced its harsh cut to my heart when my dad was taken from this life, but now I had allowed myself to become so close to you, that I knew I had exposed myself in a way I hadn't thought completely through.

You were Ireland's oldest lady but to me you were simply my best friend, and, in many ways, I thought you were going to live forever. You were the person I spent every waking minute with and for the minutes I wasn't in your company where I would go home to do a few bits there, I missed you. I would sit down at the kitchen table with mam to catch up on all her news and within a short time frame I would become unsettled. Mam would say 'I know Louise' and I would say 'What mam?', "You're unsettled Lou and you want to go back up to Gran" and I'd say "Yep I miss her, I want to go back" So instead of relaxing and just taking a break I would make my way back to Gran's earlier than I was expected. I never thought as I got closer and closer to you, that the risk of my heart being smashed into a million pieces was increasing more and more. When I was with you, I knew who I was and for the time I stepped away during the day, I hadn't a clue who I was so I couldn't wait to get back up to you. The minute I walked back in your door, everything was just as it should be again. I was your full-time carer but I never ever thought of it like that, I just thought of it as I loved you and wanted you to be happy and feel loved. I definitely think I achieved that end of my goal which gives me a lot of comfort in these days of missing you.

See I loved you from the minute I met you as my grandmother and all through those years where you showed me so much affection, I just simply loved you. My favourite trait about you was your boundless kindness for everyone you met and your good sense of humour. You were always so generous to us all in so many ways. You were famous for your fivers and equally famous for your love and listening ear. Time didn't matter to you, you always had loads of it for each of us with no limits around it. You gave love out without question and made us all feel like we were your favourite while declaring to one and all, that you had no favourites and that was true, you were a woman of your word. You believed what you said, and you said what you believed, and I loved that about you.

You made everyone feel special and you made everyone feel like they were your only focus. It was a special sort of power you had, a power where love was served out unconditionally and we all relished being in your presence because of that special superpower. It was the reason I did what I did. It was the reason I never gave up even when it was so tough during the intense lockdowns. Of course, like everyone I never thought the lockdowns were going to go on for so long and really we were just coming out of it all when you took God's hand and left me and left us all. I know I'm writing this from my perspective but I am very aware and want to reaffirm that so many people loved and cared for you. Your family first and foremost, your children, all of them and your grandchildren and extended family and friends all loved and cared for you. I know I'm in the spotlight more as I was very much active at the end of your life but I want to take this moment to reiterate that you and I both know the reason you lived so long was because so many people loved and cared for you throughout the whole of your life Gran. I know your girls and Finian and so many of the grandchildren all contributed so much to your long and happy life. Before I was here in such an intense way, so many others had sat in the seat beside you and in so many ways that is why you became such a wonderfully all-round sage of a lady and a friend to so many. So much love you gave out and so much love came back to you. And I loved that. I loved that you were so loved because that is what you deserved. In this world, most good people do not get what they deserve, but in the end, you got the passing from this world into the next in the most magical way.

And it is that, you leaving me, you leaving your beautiful family and friends in such a peaceful and serene way that I will always be grateful for. I could take care of you in lots of ways but I could not guarantee or even influence in anyway how you would leave me. You always wanted to die in your home and that was the promise I made to you when I moved in. I promised you I would do my upmost, my very best that I would not let you die out of your home, no matter what happened. I never knew what that really meant until the pandemic hit and everything became harder. But equally, everything became more magical too. The ticking of the many clocks in your kitchen will forever remind me of our very special intimate days together. Where you me, the clocks and only God knows what we shared.

You never were cross or annoyed. You never were sharp or selfish. In my time, all you wanted was cups of tea, chats, prayers, love and laughter. You were so happy in your little kitchen sitting up cosy beside the jubilee fire with the door opening and closing with so many visitors before covid landed of course.

Friends and neighbours were so important to you. I've learned so much from you on that front Gran. I've been reminded that life can indeed be short and it can indeed be very long, none of us know but to have a friend or if you are lucky to have a few friends is a real gift. I watched how you spoke to your friends, how you checked in on them, how you loved them just the way they were and you never ever spoke badly of them. I did see you disappointed on occasions, and you still didn't say a negative word. You held your ground on keeping your words of goodness one hundred per cent of the time and you were wonderfully appreciative of all who took care and interest in you. You had friendships that lasted a lifetime, and you lost a lot of friends due to you living so long.

As we both know, living long doesn't mean it's all rosy in the garden. You lost your husband, your twin daughters, your brothers and sisters, nephews and nieces all went before you, my dad went before you too at the very young age of 64. I know that took a lot out of you to keep smiling for us especially seeing my mam so devastated. But you did. You were strong and formidable in the face of all the storms that passed your way and ours too. You were the roots in our family tree and you kept us together. You kept us strong. You kept us open. You kept us going.

There is no doubt, your house, your chair, your bedroom are all very empty without you now. I still smell your clothes in your wardrobe when I'm having a really bad day. Does that help? I'm not sure but in my heart, it does. It allows me to remember and for a moment pretend you're not gone forever. I wander around the kitchen wholeheartedly broken and upset on the really lonely moments when nobody can see me but Tom the cat but what I am learning is that you may not be physically with me anymore, but my God did you keep our second promise.

In the interviewing process of this book, I'll never forget the many discussions and conversations we had about Heaven. You always said the same thing "Why does nobody come back Louise and tell us what it's like?" You used to ask me with such belief that I knew the answer. That one distinct day that we had such a deep and heart wrenched discussion, I clearly remember my reply to you, "Do you know Gran, I don't know, but what I do know is what we can do about it? For once and for all me and you can answer it for everyone else. So if I go before you to Heaven, which I very easily could, I promise I'll come back down as many times as I can with a sign for you. I'll keep coming until you believe me and until I know you know it's me giving you these signs. I'm not sure what signs I'll give you but I won't stop until you look up and say to yourself, yes that's Louise. I can still hear your reply to me Gran,"Well now Louise that's a very good plan but I hope I'm gone before you." To which I replied, "Well Gran we never know do we? So we won't worry about who goes first we will just make this promise a really serious one. We'll even shake on it and then we will finally be able to answer that question about heaven. We won't be wondering any longer, we will know. What do you think?" And on that discussion, we made our handshake to never leave each other even if we were separated physically, most importantly we would send signs galore to let each other know all about Heaven.

And my god did you keep your end of our promise Gran. The rainbows and the butterflies have been endless and so magically timed. The butterfly that landed on me on New Year's Eve here in your kitchen and decided to crawl up my shoe, all the way up my leg never mind the countless number of other butterflies who have landed on me in some shape or form. It's been quite the butterfly experience and I'm so grateful to every single one. And then when I move onto the amazing number of rainbows you have brought to my witness. I can't even put into words. The evening before you passed, a magical rainbow appeared right beside your house here. I now know that was a sign from God that he was coming to take you. I didn't know it at the time, but it certainly was because ever since, if I wobble at all or feel really lonely for you, that exact rainbow appears. Often without any rain even falling, the rainbow appears. I know it's you Gran. On top of that, the three evenings leading up to your one-year anniversary, again three more consecutive rainbows appearing right beside your house. I thank you from the bottom of my heart for the many signs you have sent and as you know, I know it's you and I'm so grateful we made that promise because it gives me great comfort to know you are okay. Actually, I know you are doing better than okay. You are doing magnificently in Heaven. You are home with so many people you love and so many people who love you and that really helps my broken heart.

The writing of this book has not been easy, but I can tell you at this stage and it's more a feeling in my heart than anything, it has been worth every tear I dropped on my keyboard. I've cried an awful lot here on my own Gran as I watched all our interviews, videos, and audio recordings to put this book together, but it's been worth it. I'm so grateful your life was captured in some way and now, forever more, you can help people from Heaven just like you did when you were on earth! Thank God I recorded everything. If anything, I've learned, the best thing to have when you lose someone is a recording of their voice. It's so comforting to feel you so close. Yes, it's upsetting but definitely over time it has given me great healing and it's just so lovely to hear you speak in your kind gentle voice. The good memories are always triggered and even with tears, that is never a bad thing. Healing comes every time a tear drops.

As I come to the end of my final letter to you Gran, I know our relationship has changed since you left for Heaven, but I feel you as close as I did when I held your hand. You were such a special person here on earth to have lived for such a long time and to have given all of your heart to every person you met, and you never lost your smile no matter how heavy life got. I count myself so lucky to have known you and that is indeed what life is all about. We are here to love with our hearts and when our time is called to leave this earth, to know we have given it our best shot and to leave a legacy of love, hope and healing behind us. You were a wonderful best friend and I know our time was given for a purpose and a reason. This book being one of them. Your beauty, glow and inner strength and spirit shines out through your joyful words and even though you are gone, in lots of ways, you will live forever. I thank you from the bottom of my heart for loving me and equally for allowing me to love you and hope that I do you proud every day of the rest of my life. I will pray to you; I will look up to you and I will always have you in my heart and for that I am eternally grateful. In life, we become the people we want to become and also, we move to the beat of the hearts of those who inspire us. You will forever inspire, and I hope, in even a little way, I will carry the goodness, the smile and the ultimate joy that you brought so many with me.

Say hello to Dad for me and all my favourite people up there. We will meet again one day and I know you will have a seat waiting beside you. Until then, thank you Granny for being you. Thank you for all the signs. And thank you for allowing me to be me too.

Forever your best friend and someone who will never forget you,

Lou x

Looking at all our memories in Gran's beautiful kitchen is a reminder of all the good times we had.

A beautiful butterfly reminding me that Gran is never far away and is minding everyone from Heaven now.

CHAPTER THIRTEEN
WHAT OTHERS FELT ABOUT GRANNY NANCY

KATHLEEN MAYE - ***Daughter***

Mum, so glad to have been part of your life and loved you for so long and watched our family love and care for you. Miss all the daily visits, chats and cups of tea. Love Kathleen x

Katheen is pictured here with her daughter Ramona and her daughter baby Alannah and Granny Nancy.

MARY YOURELL - *Daughter*

We all had our particular jobs with mum. For me it was the Christmas decorations and flowers that were my department. For the Christmas decorations the 8th of December was D Day. Decorations couldn't go up before that date. But come the 8th, the first question to me from mum was 'Have you got the decorations ready to go up?' Every year we got new ones, just in case. Every year I hung them and mum supervised. Are they straight? Are they crooked? Too long? Too Short or maybe just perfect. She loved the house decorated to a hilt. And don't even think of taking them down before the 6th of January. That was not worth your life.

Next up was the chats and pre chats about the flowers. "Maybe there will be a lull between now and the good weather. No frost is what we want."And so it's flower time. "Mary are you ready to sow the flowers? Have you got the peat moss and the pots and most importantly the flowers?" Off to the garden centre I would go and buy the usual display. They knew it was for mums house and they knew what she liked. And so the supervising started again. What to plant in what pot and where to place the flowers to get the most out of the display. She loved her flowers. She was always so grateful for everything we did for her. The privilege at the end of the day was all mine. Love Mary x

Granny pictured here with her daughter Mary on Gran's 107th Birthday.

OLIVE COGHLAN - *Daughter*

My life is not the same since you left. The days are longer without you in it, but I know you are happy in Heaven. There will not be a day I don't miss calling to you to do your tea or all our little jobs and chats together. I fondly remember how you loved when I would ask you if you were a good girl today and if you were, you could have a few jelly babies. Without fail, we would laugh every evening about the same joke. I hope you have an endless supply of sweets in Heaven now mam because you deserve them all. I'm sure you are handing them out to everyone knowing your generous nature, the angels included. No doubt you are best friends with everyone up there now and giving them all a great laugh. Five o'clock in the evening is not the same without you in it but I count myself so lucky to have had you as my mother and I have so many good memories and no regrets with all the time I spent with you. Know you and Joe are together now in Heaven and that gives me great comfort.

Lots of love, Olive x

Mam and Granny loved to chat and laugh every evening as if they hadn't seen each other in ages.

TRACY LEE - *Granddaughter*

We all loved Granny's magic tablecloth. The kids were intrigued by how no matter when we called there was always a little something waiting for them underneath it. How we all wished we had one of those in our homes. Kindness was one of her best qualities.

On a completely different note, Granny was very funny too. One day back in 2019, she told Brian my husband that she doesn't run anymore. That had to be the funniest thing she ever said. We had popped into say hello after we were out running the boreen. She asked us where were we coming from and we said "Ah just out for a run Gran" in which she then proceeded to tell us, "Oh I don't run anymore." Absolutely hilarious. Now whether this was pure mischief or maybe she really did run back in her day, we will never know now. But she was such a funny character and we all loved her.

Granny is pictured here with Tracy, Brian and their children Stewart, Ruby and Zoe Lee.

KAREN MC NEVIN - ***Carer***

It was a pleasure to know and take care of Nancy. Not too many can say they cared for a lady of her kind. She was just a unique woman in every way.

TARA CULLINANE - ***Granddaughter***

I have many great childhood memories of Granny Nancy. From being upstairs in the lumpy bed and waking up to hear my dear mum Anne and Granny Nancy supposedly whispering not to wake me and I'd say the whole parish could hear them catching up on the news in Clonard. Also Granny would have the fridge full of ham, salads, sausages etc. She eventually realised all she needed was eggs and crusty bread for the traditional egg in the cup on the range and bread toasted on one side under the grill. And of course the mug of tea to wash it down. I hope you are happy and content in Heaven with Bob [He asking is it old or new time?] and please give my love to Auntie Maggie and my dear mum Anne. Lots of love from Tara and all in Tralee xx

Granny is pictured here with her Mattie Clifford (Son in law) and his daughter Tara and her children Ben and David Cullinane.

KEN MAYE - *Grandson*

I've had so many good memories of my Granny from my childhood to her passing last year. I remember calling on her 102nd birthday, I had just celebrated my 51st year and I was in awe to see this small lady that had doubled my years, here she was older than our state, seen changes in our society that was hard to comprehend.

One constant through all that change was her indomitable spirit her vigour for life was there all the way through her life and was an inspiration for all to see.

I miss calling when I pass her home, I miss the warm welcome, the teapot drawing on the Jubliee range, the local stories and I miss leaving with an apple or an orange in my pocket feeling like a schoolboy all over again. We shall not see her like again.

Granddaughter Lisa Yourell holding the hand of Granny on her 106th Birthday

CLAIRE COGHLAN - ***Granddaughter***

Granny was a great woman and lived a great life. We all were so fond of her and miss her dearly. She reminded us all that no matter how life goes, it's important to keep good humour in the mix and eventually things work out just fine in the end.

ANTHONY AND NATHAN LOGAN - ***Great Grandchildren***

My name is Anthony and I'm 15 years old and my name is Nathan and I'm 12 years old and we loved visiting Granny after school. Granny always had lovely homemade soup for us or nice goodies she had baked. Gran was so kind and always had lots of chat for us. We miss her an awful lot and there will never be another Granny like her again. We were very lucky to have her so long.

Granny is pictured here with Claire Coghlan, Anthony Logan, Lauren Logan, Shauna Logan, Josh Logan, Nathan Logan and Anthony (Jnr.) Logan.

LAUREN LOGAN - ***Great Grandchild***

My name is Lauren. Me and Granny were very good friends because I was always one hundred years younger than Granny and that was very special. I loved Granny and she was such a special person. She's in Heaven now and she is an angel. I think she is a saint up there because she was such a good person and so many people loved her. She prayed and helped so many people here on earth. I know she can see us and if we need her help, we can just ask her and she will be listening. I miss her a lot and I know her cat Tom really misses her too.

JOSH AND SHAUNA LOGAN - *Great Grandchildren*

My name is Josh and I am six and my name is Shauna and I am five. We loved Granny so much and she always chatted to us and asked us about school and everything. We loved calling to her house and we love her cat Tom. She was a great granny.

ANTHONY LOGAN

Granny Nancy was a great woman and we always had great chats. You could sit and talk to her for hours about anything and she would have a word on every topic. She would always ask me how I was getting on driving out on the continent and what was the news out there. She was a mind of information, and you would never have guessed what age she was.

Anthony, Shauna, Nathan, Josh and Lauren Logan pictured with Granny Nancy on her 105th birthday with their mam Claire Coghlan.

JUSTIN COGHLAN - ***Grandson***

Granny was a great woman. I always had a great relationship with her and we were all very lucky to have her in our lives for so long. There sure won't be another Granny. She was one of a kind.

Justin and Granny having a great chat at her 107th Birthday

VICKI CAULFIELD - ***Carer***

Kind, funny and witty are three words that come to my mind when I fondly remember Nancy Stewart. An extraordinary lady who had a great sense of humour. We had so many laughs together especially the hairdos. You can only imagine the conversations we had. Thank you Nance for making my days brighter, my tummy sore from laughter and the joy and honour it was not only to care for you but to love and know you. I will never forget you.

MARTHA DALTON - ***Clogherinkoe, County Kildare***

I met Granny Nancy through Louise back in 2018 and a somewhat unlikely friendship grew quite quickly from that!

We both got on like a house on fire and loved when we got together as the conversation flowed between us and we had plenty of fun and laughs!

Granny was such a young at heart character and she taught me to embrace and enjoy life each and every day. She helped me become more aware of the value of 'the simple life' and how being kind to all really does make for a better world. I've no doubt she is guiding us all from above. Miss you Granny xxx

SOPHIE MARTIN - ***Clonard, County Meath***

Where do I start, Granny Nancy is such an inspiration to everyone. She shone a light in the world brighter than the sun. When Granny Nancy broke her hip and I went to visit her and she still had a smile on her face that could light up the world. No matter what the universe threw at her she always smiled, which made others smile too. When I think of Granny Nancy and the opportunity to enjoy a cuppa and a biscuit with her and enjoy listening to her incredible stories, she gave me the hope to keep going and to live my life like she lived hers, with love, light and hope.

My favourite story that Granny Nancy told me was the time she left her new leather boots in front of the stove because she didn't want to go to school wearing them. Her mam had bought her these new leather boots and she loved them but didn't want people in school to laugh at her. So she left them in front of the stove overnight to let the leather burn off so that she wouldn't have to wear them. I love this story because it gave me a good laugh when she told me about it, and that's why she is so special, because she always made others laugh and smile. Granny Nancy could never have had such an impact on people if it wasn't for her beautiful granddaughter Lou. Lou you have kept her company through thick and thin and you have never left her side, even through her darkest days. And I know you don't accept praise, but you have been an incredible best friend and granddaughter to Granny Nancy, and the only reason she lived as long as she did was because of you. You never stopped going, even when times were tough and you are both just incredible! You will both forever be an inspiration and a light to others and I will never be able to express in words how much you both mean to me.
Soph x - Age 15

NANCY

By San Connolly

This wonderful Lady Nancy,
Lived through so many tough times,
Her faith carried her forward,
Her prayers and her rhymes.

Her friendly sweet voice,
Her cheeky soft grin,
Was only a snippet,
Of the powerful lady within.

Rearing a family,
Her grandkids in toe,
All the world loved her,
Of that I'm sure she did know.

She had so many skills,
She sure had a lot,
And if you called in for tea,
Your name was put in the pot.

A cake and a scone,
Was offered with care,
This dear little lady,
From her heart she would share.

You'd never go hungry,
That she would not allow,
If she didn't have milk,
She'd send you out to the cow.

Her humour and wit,
It carried her through,
All of life's challenges,
Of which only she knew.

When you think of dear Nancy,
And I'm sure that you will,
Put on your best smile,
Be happy and still.

You'll feel her warm presence,
Her warmth and her flare,
This wonderful woman,
In your heart will always be there. Look up xxxx

MARY HAND

I didn't know Granny Nancy, but I feel like I did. I would have loved to have talked to her personally. She was an amazing lady.

FIONA HIGGINS

I didn't know Granny Nancy personally either but with all the stories and videos you shared with us I feel like I knew her so well.

MARJORIE LORD

I loved my visits to Granny Nancy. She was so grateful and always full of life. You always left her fulfilled and feeling a lot better. She was very chatty and had lovely stories from her youth. It was a great experience to have had the privilege of spending time with her. I miss her. Rest in peace Granny Nancy.

OLI LYNCH MONAGHAN

Granny Nancy brought sunshine to dark days with her faith, her inspirational words and her amazing zest for life. A truly wonderful lady.

JOY DRISCOLL - ***Pennsylvania, USA.***

Living alone in Pennsylvania, USA with no family around I spend considerable time on Facebook. One day a smiling face popped up sitting in a chair holding her rosary beads with a very chatty girl by her side. I immediately fell in love with the love being portrayed in front of me. Oh, how I wish I could have sat in for a cuppa or to listen to mass with these delightful long lost unrelated relatives.

Every day I was invited into a loving, sometimes zany, sometimes painful or sacred circle just by showing up and even was greeted by dear sweet

Lou verbally. I loved our trips to the empty churches to light a candle for us all or to the cemetery to all cry for our losses but then she'd say, "Keep looking up" and find a way to sooth my broken heart. I'll never visit my dear friend across the pond, but my heart makes the trip every day. We all lost Granny Nancy with you and prayed through your pain and exhaustion as you cared for the other half of your soul. Thank you for popping into my life out of the blue. I love you xx

ANNE O'MARA

I met Granny Nancy a long time ago and met her again at the Bush Mass in Clogherinkoe years later, and she remembered me. She was such an amazing lady, and a lovely lady at that.

Smiling for the camera, the two ladies who laughed and lived together.

ANNA MORAN - *UK*

Being introduced to you and Granny Nancy through Facebook in 2020 has been such an inspiration. From enjoying each day with you both, I was reminded how blessed [especially through lockdown] to have family friends and to live life to the full. Also to love my Irish connections. God Bless you and Granny Nancy. Every time I see rainbows, butterflies and triangular groups of birds it's makes me so appreciate life and all the good things. What a beautiful angel your Granny Nancy was, just like you have said so many times Lou -So Blessed to have had her in your life -107 wow what an achievement x

Granny at her 106th Birthday mass in which she smiled for weeks after saying it was the loveliest thing that ever happened her. Photo by Elaine McCrossan.

VERONICA CASSIDY BARRY - *New York*

Reflections of my time with Louise Coghlan and Granny Nancy

Who would think something good could come out of something as unprecedentedly horrific as a global pandemic? Certainly, I didn't.

I am not sure exactly how I met Louise and Granny Nancy Stewart, but the second I did they made me feel like family. The COVID-19 lockdown in New York City began around St. Patrick's Day 2020. The first week seemed like it would be fun; like a snow day - no work and no school. But, almost immediately, my daughters' school lost two beloved members of the staff. Soon after, we lost an elderly relative and a younger cousin. There were no wakes, no funerals, no hugs. No human contact - at all. It became clear that we would not be returning to normal any time soon.

In May of 2020, I found Louise Coghlan and her Granny Nancy! I thank God I did. Life became scary and depressing, the pressure of trying to keep optimistic was taking a toll on all of us.

Louise and Granny Nancy managed to pull us up when we were losing hope. Louise, with her enthusiastic joy for life, her vast selection of inspirational music and empathy, reached across the globe and touched our hearts. She created a community of wonderful people who truly care about each other. With Granny Nancy as her inspiration, Louise reminded us to be thankful for each day and be thankful for each other.

During the early days of lockdown, the community that Louise created leaned on each other. We prayed together, we laughed together, we cried together. 'Lou' as we have come to call her, kept us smiling and 'Granny Nancy', who added us to her never-ending rosaries, made us feel like cousins. Louise and Granny Nancy even called me on video one morning. It was such a gift. Still struggling with the loss of my own parents, it was so wonderful to know that such a saintly woman with her warm motherly presence was thinking of me and remembering me in her prayers.

Lou brought us together once, twice - sometimes three times a day. Quite often these Facebook live sessions were the only thing to look forward to, and I am so grateful for each one. We celebrated the tiniest joys and mourned the biggest losses. Lou introduced us to her; local parish, community, family, neighbours - even Mags, who regularly delivered mail during our chats. Broadford, Enfield, Clonard and Kinnegad became household names.

The entire time Lou was giving to all of us, she was spending her time as a companion and caretaker to her best friend, Granny Nancy. Some days we worried about Louise. We wondered if she was doing ok and where she got her energy. The scariest moments were when Granny Nancy had health scares, but she always rallied and we were overjoyed to celebrate her 107th birthday together.

In the year that followed, we shared a few live calls, several of our own birthday celebrations, hundreds of Facebook lives, and many, many Hail Marys. We looked forward to celebrating Granny Nancy's 108th birthday together, but sadly Granny Nancy was taken to heaven. We cried with and for her family - especially our dear, Louise. We joined the funeral from around the world and hoped that Louise could feel the love from across the miles. We were in awe when Lou delivered such an eloquent speech at her Granny's grave - but [that is our Lou!] Louise Coghlan is Granny Nancy's legacy.

Lou inherited Granny Nancy's goodness and strength - I am so grateful to them both for sharing their gifts with all of us. You have made such a difference in our lives and are both so very loved.

EMBY FOOTE

Granny Nancy: a woman of faith always saying her prayers with her rosary beads in her hand. Like women of her age her religion was very important to her. Always looked like the Queen all done up with her lipstick and lovely pearls and hats. Like so many women of her age loved to bake the bread and tarts. I just loved reading all about her and what an amazing person she was. Love and hugs to you Louise.

CARMEL MC TAGGART

I did not know much about your Granny Nancy when I joined the 'Living and Laughing with Lou' Facebook page. I only seen her a few times, but I can say she has made an amazing lady out of you. Your gentle, kind and amazing heart, you get from her and you touch people's life's in ways that is so rare so as far as I'm concerned Granny Nancy will go on in you. God bless you. I can't wait to read her book.

DAISY AND ROSE CAREY - ***Celtic Blondes Dancers***

We were absolutely delighted to meet Granny Nancy at the Clonard Vintage and Heritage Club's Annual Vintage Show in 2013. It was a joy to speak to Nancy, and to hear how much she enjoyed the music and dancing that was taking place at the Vintage Show. We also had a lovely chat to Granny Nancy's granddaughter, Louise, who we have been friends with for many years. We fondly remember Granny Nancy, and her zest for life.

Granny pictured with beautiful Daisy and Rose of the Celtic Blondes

MARGARET STAFFORD

For me Louise and Granny Nancy epitomises all that was good in the Ireland of old - Family values, deep faith, great gratitude despite her hardships and the ability to look ahead regardless of age or health. She had a great acceptance of life's ups and downs. She just went with the flow. Lots of these attributes I envy. We have lost lots in our high-speed modern world and I think her simplicity struck a deep chord with so many people. Best of luck with the whole adventure Lou. You're a Star. She's always with you. Hugs, Granny Mags aka Margaret Stafford x

MARY CASSIDY KENNEDY - ***Morristown, New Jersey, USA***

The story of Louise and Granny Nancy is a multi-faceted love story, that started long before they became a viral sensation; One that's been approximately 109 years in the making.

Although my chapter in their story is brief in comparison to the rest of the story, the impact they have had in my life will endure.

I had the pleasure of meeting Granny Nancy and Louise, in the early cocooning days. While people worldwide were suffering the effects of disease, loss, and isolation, this petite centenarian and her granddaughter invited the world into Granny's cottage in Clonard, Kinnegad, to share a cup of tea, have a chat, sing a song, and say a prayer.

Smiling behind their masks, they welcomed us in virtually, but soon real-life friendships developed. Soon, Granny Nancy became everyone's Granny, with lessons to impart. Every lesson taught by example, accompanied by compassion and reassurance that everything will be okay.

Granny's greatest lesson was that of resilience-bolstered by faith and prayers of both petition and gratitude. Granny prayed several hours each day. She prayed for loved ones in heaven and on earth, family and friends, old and new, and many people she never met. She reminded us that this is what helped her survive many painful challenges, including wars, pandemics, loss of her beloved husband Bob, and then her twin daughters, Margaret and Anne.

She knew that every day spent on this earth was a gift; Even when her frail health brought her close to death many times, she chose to rally back and carry on, with the help of her loving support network, made up of her granddaughter Louise, daughter Olive, and her carers.

Through it all she never lost her faith; in fact, it only grew stronger. During some of the darkest days of the Covid-19 pandemic, Granny taught people who did not know how to pray, encouraged those who may have forgotten the words, and prayed for those who did not have the strength to pray on their own. She and Louise even led the Rosary on Radio Maria, as people joined in from all over the world. She believed in the power of prayer, the communion of saints and everlasting life in Heaven. Nancy and Louise's 'Letter of Hope' was read with the tune, 'Give Me Your Hand' [Tabhair dom do lámh] playing in the background. The chorus of the song has taken on new meaning for me as I reflect upon the unconditional love and care that Louise provided, with an image in my mind of Louise holding her Granny's hand. Louise's dedication and instincts undoubtedly prolonged Nancy's joy-filled life;

"By day and night throughout struggle and strife,
I'm beside you to guide you forever my love.
For love's not for one but for both of us to share,
For this country so fair for our world and what's there."

Thank you, Louise and Granny Nancy, for sharing your story and for inviting friends worldwide to become a part of Nancy Stewart's lasting Legacy of Love. We will continue to keep all of you in our prayers, confident in the hope, that one day we will all be reunited.
Love Always,
Mary Cassidy Kennedy

**Songwriters: Andrew Goldstein / Jordan Witzigreuter / Simon Wilcox*
Give Me Your Hand lyrics © Peermusic Publishing, Sony/ATV Music Publishing LLC, Warner Chappell Music, Inc

JOAN KELLY - *Celbridge, County Kildare*

Dearest Louise, Joan Kelly here in Celbridge. Granny Nancy - what can I say. Sadly, I never got to meet her in person. I got to know her through Facebook. What an amazing lady. She's a legend. I had contacted Granny Nancy through her lovely granddaughter Louise. It was October 2020. Our beautiful mammy, our queen bee Lillie Byrne was turning ninety two on the 26th of that October. Mammy was unwell, and as she had caught Covid. She was feeling very low. As we were all not able to be in with her, Granny Nancy sent my mam a beautiful video with such wit and words of encouragement. It really meant so much to us all. Mammy was delighted with it. We were so grateful we got it and she got to see it as sadly mammy passed away two days after her birthday.

Nancy was such a selfless woman, so kind and witty, full of fun and gave so much hope to people. She lives on through her amazing Louise. Even though she's going through her own grief of losing Nancy, Lou gives hope, encouragement and lifts peoples spirits every day. I will be forever grateful.

Lots of love, Joan Kelly x

Granny and I celebrating our interview with EWTN hitting one million views. That clip now stands at over five million views - the population of Ireland!

ANNETTE O' ROURKE

You have always spoken from the heart with such love about Nancy, that we all came to know and love her too. I included her letter in last year's First Holy Communion Booklet 2021 as a keepsake for the children. She was such a wonderful soul beyond words. God Bless, Annette.

NANCY KELLY - *London*

Dear Louise, I would like to thank you for allowing me speak with Granny Nancy. What a wonderful gift and memory you gave to me. I will never forget that call and I will always ask Granny Nancy to keep my Derry in her prayers and to help us as he battles a terrible time of illness. God bless you, Nancy and Derry xx

NORAH MONAGHAN - *Navan, County Meath*

It is very thoughtful of you to include the Facebook family in your book. While I'm not gifted with words, I know for sure that Granny Nancy kept me sane especially during the lockdowns. To see this strong, understanding lady of one hundred and seven able to tolerate the dreadful lack of visitors, to be isolated and wearing masks. I was very lucky that I didn't get the virus, and I went walking in the park every day. As I walked, I thought of this elderly lady and how she held her head up and dealt with her suffering with a smile. It made my day easier to live with as we were all struggling to keep our sanity. God bless you Louise for being so generous with your time. I hope all goes well for you in life.

GERALDINE BOLAND

2020 our lives came to a standstill. When all seemed doom and gloom, a beautiful life angel 'Granny Nancy' and her beautiful granddaughter Louise came onto Facebook. And all was well again. Your laughter, prayers, cooking, chats kept us all going. Good days and bad days, you brought us through them all. A hundred thousand thanks to you both. And Granny Nancy will live on forever in our hearts and lives. Thank you Louise for everything x

DENISE CUSACK SCHNEIDER - *Moyvalley, County Kildare*

In my eyes, Nancy is a saint. Her presence was unique. Being with Nancy in her lovely, charming home with a cup of tea was like nothing you can buy. It was good for the soul. Her smiles and eyes showed constant kindness.

When I was pregnant in 2020, with little Rosie [before Covid], Nancy put her gentle hand on my bump - to me that was a magical moment.
Myself, Louise and Nancy sat around drinking tea, laughing and we all use her 'Oil of Olay' cream on our faces which she swore by. Her skin was unreal.

She loved my mam's Rosaleen Cusack brown bread and loved planting tomatoes with my dad Michael Cusack. She was an all-rounder who never let age get in her way of enjoying life. Laughter. Fried bread and sausages. Fair City. These are a few words that come to mind when I remember Nancy, but genuinely the main word is 'kindness'. It was an absolute honour knowing Nancy Stewart.

LAUREN DEBORAH - *Writer, Canada*

While I never had the honour of meeting Granny Nancy, I sense her spirit enormously in Lou. I feel the friendship, the positivity, the kindness, the faith, the openness, the humour, the love and the hope all come through

Lou to spread the messages that meant the world to Granny Nancy. These are the things that kept her living in bliss for one hundred and seven years. These are the things that Lou embodies in every interaction - no matter how big or small, no matter friend or stranger - Lou epitomises the traits that made Granny Nancy the amazing woman she was.

That is why there is no better person to tell Granny Nancy's story than Lou. They are granddaughter and grandmother, who were also best friends and kindred spirits. They hold a special bond I have never witnessed and share the kind of love we all deserve. This story will bring you exactly what you are searching for.

DENISE MARTIN - ***Clonard, County Meath***

We first had the pleasure of meeting Granny in February 2019. Myself and two of my kids Sophie and Ryan went to visit her in the nursing home where she was recovering from her hip operation. She was so welcoming and friendly. We enjoyed her stories of old days and her good humour and wit. We had a cup of tea and a biscuit and she even insisted sharing her sweets with us. To tell the truth we didn't want to leave. We visited more when she got back home to her gorgeous cottage and even shared in her 106th and 107th birthday celebrations. Her 107th birthday was during Covid so we took part in her drive by birthday. We were having so much fun we drove by her house three times beeping. Granny, you are an inspiration to us all. Such an amazing person and you live on in my good friend Louise, your granddaughter. I know you would be so proud of her writing and publishing this book. It was a pleasure meeting you and thank you Louise for letting us all be a part of her life x

MARTHA BERGIN

So lovely to find nice normal people enjoying each other's company and sharing with the rest of us. Giving encouragement to us during difficult times for all of us. Thank you so much for that Lou x

DAMIEN ROONEY - ***Mullingar, County Westmeath***

Granny Nancy had a monthly appointment in the Eye and Ear Hospital, Dublin to check her eyes. One of those times I was elected to drive her. Early that morning, I collected Nancy and her daughter Mary from Enfield. Granny Nancy was no longer able to see where we were on the road but, by God, she knew where we were. Every time we passed something of significance, she would tell a story. I later discovered these stories were a regular part of her Eye and Ear adventure.

She went in for her check-up and I went for coffee until the ladies were ready to be collected.
"How did you get on?" I asked, when I collected them. "Ah, great," Nancy replied. "The nurses are lovely there."
"Granny, do you know what was there before the Eye and Ear Hospital?" I asked.
"No . . ."
I replied, "A site for sore eyes."
It took a minute but then she got it, bursting into a hearty laugh. She got it again at Lucan, at Maynooth and at Kilcock. When she got out of the car in Enfield, she thanked me for the lift, still laughing and repeating the words. "A site for sore eyes."

MARIAN KNIPE - ***Cookstown, County Tyrone***

I can't remember exactly when I came on your page but I know that it was exactly when I needed it!! Lockdown and everything was getting on top of me and here comes this beautiful lady Louise and her legend of a Granny lifting all our spirits. The wee random video calls meant more than you will ever know. I feel so blessed to have met you. One of a kind and without you we would never have known the amazing Nancy.

EITHNE M MCGARRITY - ***Cookstown, County Tyrone***

I only found 'Living and Laughing with Lou' after the loss of her beloved Granny Nancy. I had known of the amazing 107 year old Nancy Stewart, so I was intrigued to hear Louise's stories. Her warm heart and inspiring words drew me in, and I learned more about Granny Nancy and the amazing duo they had been for so many during lockdown.

Louise has been so honest through her grieving process. Her wisdom, inspiring words, kindness and love for the 'Facebook Family' has undoubtedly lightened many a sad heart. You are a great person like your Granny before you, a rare jewel to treasure as a friend. Love from Cookstown in County Tyrone x

GRANNY NANCY

By Maura McCreave

I never had the privilege of meeting Granny Nancy,
But seeing pics and watching vids
I know she was quite fancy!

A heart of gold, so I've been told,
Her legacy is Lou,
Her grandchild who has dedicated,
All her life to you.

And she still does from down below,
While you are up above,
Supporting our Facebook family,
With your greatest gift of love.

She has inherited your loving streak,
Welcoming old and young,
You have started something special Nancy,
Lou's new life, just begun.

This book now written in your honour,
Is testament of her love,
And as we look up we can almost feel,
Butterfly kisses from above.

And as Lou would say... keep looking up,
We find you in rainbow and sun,
The butterfly, the robin,
A friend to everyone.

I hope you've donned your dancing shoes,
In Heaven up above,
As my gentleman Jim will waltz with you,
And dance to the end of love.

YVONNE MCCULLAGH

All I can say is you both most certainly got me through a rough time with covid and brightened up my day on the following days and months and every day since. I still have a great belief she's still with us. Sure aren't you keep us all strong Lou and thank you x

EMMA RHIND TUTT - ***Writer, UK***

I didn't know you Louise when Granny Nancy was alive but after our chat the other week I felt so good about myself for days and days after. Pure magic! I never feel good about myself that way normally, and if that's your Granny Nancy's spirit I'm sorry I didn't get to meet her in person but goodness does that spirit live on in you!

JOANIE HUTCHINSON

She was everybody's Granny with her beautiful words of wisdom and all her prayers. Thank you for sharing her with us Louise x

JULIE BIRCHALL - ***Bedfordshire***

Joanie, that's exactly how I felt too.

CAROLINE HORGAN - ***Cork***

Just a big thank you Lou for sharing with us all your beautiful memories with Granny Nancy. You are an inspiration to us all.

MARY O'NEILL

Thank you Granny Nancy and Lou for helping us all come through the last couple of years with your happy smiles and positivity. You have been a breath of fresh air. We all miss Granny Nancy, but Louise is keeping her spirit alive. X

MARCELLA MCKEOWN

Your posts with Granny Nancy kept us all sane during the lockdowns. Ye were both so positive. Thank you.

SUSAN CARBERRY - ***Nottinghamshire, UK***

A very heartfelt look on life and loss and strength of the human spirit in being able to come through and smile again. It's been a spiritual journey with you Lou x

NUALA O'NEILL

Granny Nancy and Louise gave us a much needed lift during lockdown. You both cheered us up and we still look forward to the daily posts from Louise. Be very proud Granny of Louise! She is a wonderful person in every way. So lucky to know her x

We received a beautiful gift of a jigsaw from Ash Cully during the lockdown and Gran absolutely loved it. So much laughter and fun had.

KAREN BROLLY

After three heart breaking years of losing loved ones one year after another, Covid hit us in 2020. Myself and my daughter ended up being really ill with it, our lives put on hold, the whole world in lockdown and being smacked in the face with redundancy, we were trying so hard to remain calm and keep our faith, but the only person that could bring me calm was in Heaven. I thought if mum was sitting in front of me now what would she say? She would make me a cup of tea and let me pour my heart out and tell me to keep the faith, have a good night's rest and she will pray for me. And my mum's prayers were always heard. A true beautiful Irish mum. Then one day I was scrolling through my Facebook page crying and this beautiful wee Irish lady popped into my life giving me the best advice since my mum. It was Granny Nancy telling us all to keep looking up, say our prayers, to keep following the rules, to stay safe and that this wouldn't last forever. Better days are coming and she would pray for us all. She made me instantly feel calm and at ease and from then on, I wanted to hear more of Granny Nancy's advice and her beautiful outlook on life. You Louise and your Granny have been and still are a lifeline, a ray of hope, so God bless you both for always making the rainbows come out after the rain. Sending all my love to you Lou. Keep looking up, Karen x

TRACY O'BRIEN - ***Writer, Isle of Wight, UK***

I sadly never met Granny Nancy while she was still with us. But she managed to arrange for us to meet and create a friendship, for that I am very grateful. Love you lots Lou x

MARY MANGAN - ***County Offaly***

So beautiful to have you and Granny Nancy to help us to get through some difficult times. All the prayers and chat. You have been wonderful Louise. Granny Nancy will be so proud of you and we are so grateful to have you in our lives x

THERESA LANHAM

Hi Louise. I had the pleasure of meeting you at a course in Stradbally in county Laois. You often mentioned Granny Nancy in our conversations, and it was very clear you and Nancy were very close. We learned a lot about Nancy from your posts on Facebook. I do not remember my own Granny, but I felt I was part of Nancy's family. You were blessed to have had the chance to care for her at home. No matter how long you have them for it is still a terrible loss when they pass. You have lovely memories and thanks for sharing them with us. Kind Regards, Theresa Lanham.

LOUISE DUNPHY

During the pandemic when life was rough, I couldn't get into my parents' house for three months, only to drop everything at their door and chat to them through a letterbox. I came home to find Granny Nancy and Lou on the phone. It brought back all the memories of my late grandmother, which brought a lot of smiles. Thank you for that Lou. Be very proud of all that you have done Lou and continue to do and please god my nanny is as proud of me as Nancy is of you! Best of luck with the book x

BLATHNAID DUNNE

Lou and Granny Nancy you both gave us fun, inspiration and hope during all the lockdowns. You built a community of people when it was needed and beyond that time. I felt like I was a member of your family and I'll be forever grateful for that feeling.

VALERIE NEARY

Yourself and your lovely Granny and your beautiful words over a cuppa brought comfort to me after my own mam passed away on January 26th 2021. I came across you on Facebook shortly after that date and you have helped me greatly to cope.

A special thanks to Elaine Mc Crossan and Tony McCreanor for taking so many beautiful pictures of Granny over the years and of course for all the laughs and friendships!

ELAINE MCCROSSAN - ***Photographer***

Granny Nancy was the best in my career to photograph. I started taking her photo on her 100th birthday. She never ceased to amaze me how patient she was with everybody wanting to be in a photo with her. I will always remember Tony saying to Nancy on her birthday that she had more medals in a row than the Dubs. She got a great laugh from that. We have a photo on my kitchen wall with Nancy. I think it was her 103rd birthday. It was such a privilege to be asked to take her photos on her birthdays. We loved every moment of it. Elaine and Tony x

MARGARET BURKE - ***An Post***

Nancy Stewart was part of my postal route for 15 years. Nancy's front door is where I have all my treasured memories. I would encounter Nancy heading to the Active Retirement in Clonard Hall with a friend or coming home from shopping with her family or she might be heading out for dinner, you would never know where Nancy would be off to. Another activity at the front door which I will always fondly remember was Nancy attending to her lovely flowers. Nancy would also leave a note on her front door when she needed letters posted which read, 'Margaret ring the bell' in which I got to pop in to Nancy's beautiful home where a chat, a cup of tea or a bowl of soup on colder days were waiting for me. Nancy's kindness and lovely home will be forever in my heart. A true kind, heart warming lovely lady Nancy Stewart.

MARTINA DOCKERY

Yes, I just loved checking in with Louise and what a great bunch of people are in this community. Well done on getting to this stage with having the book written. I know it will be an outstanding success and a fitting tribute to lovely Granny Nancy.

ANNE MALONEY

I don't remember how I stumbled upon you but I'm glad I did.

MARGARET WALLACE

Granny Nancy and Lou gave so many people whether far or near away their positive outlook in a very negative time. A massive thank you from everyone x

GREG COMMINS - *Longwood*

I was lucky enough to meet an amazing lady by the name of Nancy, aka Granny Nancy. I met Granny Nancy for the first time back in 2018, when I turned up on 18th October for Longwood Credit Union's recognition of its youngest and oldest members.

At that time, Granny Nancy was an incredible one hundred and five years of age. I was greeted by her warm smile and friendly handshake. We had a good chat about many things with her memory as fresh as anything. Meeting Granny Nancy was a wonderful experience, and I could feel the warmth and kindness in her presence. Not a bad word to say on anything and such a positive person. "Being kind to each other" was one of the things that Granny Nancy promoted. To finish up our conversation, I was lucky enough to take a selfie together. A year later, celebrations got underway for Granny Nancy's 106th Birthday, which I was delighted to get invited to along with many family and friends from near and far.

My memory of Granny Nancy is a treasured one and it connected me to her family, when I was delighted to meet Louise 'Lou' and her Mam Olive. Lou has taken Granny Nancy on the airwaves and onto daytime tv, where she became a celebrity across Ireland, UK and the world. She certainly is proud of Lou and finally turning the dream into a reality in publishing this book.

I wish you every success and best wishes for the future Lou. Thank you.

ERLA AND DAVID FRASER

Hope you are doing well. I never had the privilege of knowing Granny Nancy as I joined the group just before her death but was always intrigued after listening to an interview she gave when she was 106 and at the start of the pandemic. However, I've got to know her granddaughter fairly well and she does give us all hours of enjoyment and fun. It is very evident that Granny left Louise a great legacy of knowledge and a great personal outlook on life which I draw great strength and comfort from each time I listen to her live videos. Lots of Love, David and Erla x

PATRICIA GRANAHAN

I can't remember how exactly I first came across Granny Nancy and you Louise but the joy and escape you created at such a strange time. You were like sunshine on a cloudy day. From the first clip I saw, I just fell in love with this beautiful lady, Granny Nancy. Her manner, her positivity, her wise and kind words to all of us who listened so intently and Nancy's pure love for the simple things in life. From baking bread to the joy of watching her enjoy her beautiful cup of tea made with utter love by her wonderful granddaughter Lou. How privileged we were to be allowed into your world, Lou and Nancy and how grateful we are that you opened up that beautiful world to us. Granny Nancy reminded me so much of my dear mammy and her unfaltering faith and gentleness. Thanks so much for that Louise x

Gran, myself and mam in Longwood Credit Union for Gran's 105th Birthday as she was celebrated as the oldest member of Enfield Credit Union.

LILY GALVIN - *Ardagh, County Longford*

During the first lockdown I went on Facebook one day out of pure boredom, and there pops up on my timeline Granny Nancy and Lou doing a live video after making soda bread. Well from there I was hooked. Couldn't wait for every live and video. From prayers with Granny Nancy on her way to bed at night to the little chats with Lou in the kitchen afterwards. The ice-cream nights, the drinks/cuppa nights to the celebrations for Granny Nancy's birthday. I could go on all day. You may be gone from our sight Granny Nancy but by gosh you'll never be forgotten! The little signs you send, with your rainbows and robins and everything in between. You left a massive part of you to us all in your fabulous granddaughter Lou and we'll be forever grateful to you for bringing Lou to us all to keep us looking up! Sending love and hugs to Heaven today and every day. Lots of love, your friend Lilly, xxx

MELISSA WEIDMANN - *Writer, Cape Codd, USA*

In this time of fake news and fibbing politicians, we are hungry for the authentic, for the unvarnished courage of showing up as we truly are. Louise Coghlan is a shining example, illuminating the act of caring for a loved one as heroic. Whether it's about sharing a cup of tea, a butterfly landing on the windowsill or a walk in the bucolic Irish countryside, her stories will inspire you to notice the glory of simple things. And she'll remind you that grief and love are deeply intertwined gifts, honoring and applying the needed wisdom of our elders.

PAT MCLOUGHLIN

Knowing Nancy as a close friend was so special, she was such an inspirational lady. Her positive outlook on life was so refreshing she had a great confidence and love for young people and they were drawn to Nancy who always had a loving embrace for them.

Nancy was many things to many people and the Nancy I knew and loved was a lady who was full of fun and 'divilment'. The stories of her youth and of community life were amazing and the thread that weaved through the fabric of her life was one of love and dedication to family and community. Everyone who was blessed and had the good fortune of knowing such a lady could only bask in the bright rays of her love. I always felt so privileged to have shared precious time with Nancy. It was a richness beyond my dreams x.

Gran pictured with her daughters Mary, Kathleen, Olive and son Finian

Butterflies have not only visited me in my loneliest moments while writing this book but so many of them have tried and managed to land on me.

Granny is pictured here in St. Finian's Church in Clonard in which she attended mass regularly. She also loved every second of her 106th birthday mass here in which her friends, neighbours and community turned out in huge numbers to celebrate her!

CHAPTER FOURTEEN

SOME WELL KNOWN FRIENDS OF GRANNY NANCY

EDDIE ROWLEY - ***Showbiz Editor, Sunday World Newspaper***

It's a blessing when you get the opportunity to meet a special human, and I felt privileged to spend some time chatting with Nancy about her remarkable life and times a couple of years ago for a Sunday World feature.

Nancy was 106-years-old at the time, yet I could see that she still had the passion and enthusiasm of a teenager for living life to the full. "To tell you the truth, I don't think I'm that age in my mind," she explained.

I could also see that the ageing process had taken its toll on her mobility, but her mind was still razor sharp, a fact she was very grateful for. "I'm lucky I haven't got dementia as that's a terrible thing altogether. God save me from that," she said.

Nancy was our link to Irish social and political history. When she was born in 1913, the Brits ruled Ireland. She remembered the Black and Tans calling to her home during the War of Independence. She was hiding in the fields with her siblings at the time.

She grew up without electricity, running water, a bathroom, telephone, TV or car, but saw Ireland become one of the most modern and richest countries in Europe.

Thanks to her devoted and loving granddaughter, Louise, Nancy kept pace with the rapid changes in her twilight years. She was able to make her mark by connecting with people in the modern age on social media platforms such as Facebook and YouTube until the end of her days.

I found Nancy to be a gentle woman with a sunny nature. Full of joy, her positivity was refreshing and uplifting in a world of negativity. Nancy had a simple motto in life: 'Be kind to each other.' She charmed all who encountered her and was truly one of a kind.

FR. BRYAN SHORTALL - ***National Director for the Padre Pio Apostolate***

We set up the rosary on Facebook because many people were scared during the pandemic and the first lockdown in March 2020, and because we couldn't gather for Mass. Some grandmothers I knew in Dublin were saying the Rosary together on Facebook each evening and sharing their broadcast. One of them called me up, I was Parish Priest in Priorswood at that time, and asked me would I join in, and I said yes. Fr. Bill came on board and played some music as part of the Rosary, and I would have a chat with the people afterwards. We often had up to 250 plus on each night. It was a wonderful online community, but it was all that we had at the time.

I linked up with Louise Coghlan on one of those evenings and of course the wonderful Granny Nancy, who was over 100 years praying the Rosary and was praying with us. We all met Granny Nancy thanks to a programme made by another friend, Colm Flynn of EWTN and RTE. I was privileged to have a chat with her on the phone and it was wonderful to speak to her and hear how real the good Lord was to her and how readily she would "thank God and his blessed mother and all the saints" I remain grateful to God for meeting Louise and being introduced to a mighty woman who lived through many generations.

When Granny Nancy tiptoed into heaven, Louise told us the news, and while there was a sadness at her passing, we all gave thanks to God for a long life of faith, devotion, love, and witness. As Louise often reminds us, she reaches out to us every day in prayer from Heaven and asks us not to forget to pray ourselves and to stay close to the old faith - and the cup of tea and the chat.

CLIONA HAGAN - ***Irish Country Singer***

After singing at the Rose of Tralee festival I was on a high. I've always wanted to sing at that festival and to have done so was a dream come true. I got to meet so many wonderful people that night after the show but as I was standing on my lonesome, ready to hop into the van a lovely woman came out of nowhere and shyly said hello.

Instantly I knew this lady was special. I always feel like I have a superpower in sussing people's aura and I immediately knew this lady was special. She exuded such a kindness and humbleness that made her light shine so bright. Even though a two hour gig takes every ounce of energy out of my being, I could not stop talking to this lady. She started to tell me about her Granny and how she was not only the oldest woman to live but how much of a rockstar she was. I was so intrigued having had such a closeness to my Granny also. I asked her if her Gran told her the secret of life and instantly she said Cliona you already said it! I said did I? And I asked what was it that I said? She said her Granny said 'balance' was the secret of life. Work to live, not live to work! I was just mesmerised by this. Anyway the wonderful lady I met that night was called Louise, Lou for short.

For having spent only a short five minutes chatting to her she has made an impact in my life and I hope to be friends for a long time. For me, it wasn't getting to sing on that big stage at the Rose of Tralee that night, but I'll always remember that night getting to meet Lou for the first time.

Meeting you at the Rose of Tralee was my highlight too Cliona!
Here's to a lifetime of friendship

ANNE MARIE KELLY - *Broadcaster and Award Winning Documentary Maker*

So I met Granny Nancy when she turned one hundred years of age and instantly, I fell in love with her. Her home, the nooks and crannies, the tea, the fire, the glow, particularly the glow of her lovely face. I had just lost my mother and she reminded me of her in many ways. The smiling wrinkles around her eyes, the way she held herself with pride and her old fashioned way of thinking reminded me of her. Granny Nancy was the heart and her heart was wide open to strangers like me. She even allowed me to call her Granny, I'm sure I wasn't the only stranger who called her that. I kept going back for more 101, 102 birthdays and so on!

On one birthday, I brought my two little girls with me and we recorded something very special. My youngest, Mollie was 100 years younger than her yet they connected instantly. Grace, my older girl, had asked her classmates to put together questions for Nancy. They varied from ''Do you remember the Titanic?' to 'Did you use toilet paper back then?' The girls particularly loved this question as did Nancy who told them she actually didn't. There were no scripted questions from me with Nancy and that's why we loved her. There was no script and no agenda, just a genuinely beautiful soul. We miss you Nancy!

Anne Marie Kelly and Granny formed such a close bond over the years and I've been blessed with a lifetime of friendship with Annemarie also! Thank you Anne Marie for helping us spread the good news of Granny Nancy!

FR. RICHARD GIBBONS - *Parish Priest and Rector of Knock Shrine*

Nancy Stewart was a very special lady and we all knew it. Pandemics are never good, but sometimes good things come from bad times. Granny Nancy was that good thing for a lot of us. When I learned that she was tuning into mass here in Knock through our Facebook page, I knew this was a special woman as she was one hundred and seven years of age and was still reaching out to her faith through technology.

When I shared her story as part of my homily at our Sunday mass in August 2021, the reaction to it was exceptional. The story of Granny Nancy touched the hearts of so many, myself included. She was a wonderful christian with a very kind outlook on life and no doubt she will be remembered forever more as the lady who stood forward with a bright light as darkness fell on our country and our world.

Rest in Peace Granny Nancy Stewart and thank you for your inspiring faith and hope and we pray that you are now in the loving embrace of God.

LUAN PARLE - *Irish Musician and Songwriter*

I first met beloved Granny Nancy in 2008 through her granddaughter Louise. Louise had interviewed me for an article for a newspaper while she was working as a journalist, and we immediately hit it off and very quickly became the best of friends. I remember visiting Louise at her family home, and Granny Nancy had popped over with some hot apple tarts that she had baked and offered me a slice with a cup of tea. It was the most delicious apple tart I had ever tasted. She was the most wonderful, warm, incredible lady, and we had great conversations around the kitchen table that day. In April 2020, when everybody was isolating at home with their loved ones due to COVID and the restrictions imposed, I called Louise and Granny Nancy to ask them if they would help me out and take part in a video for a single I was releasing. I was delighted when they agreed. They sent me the most marvellous footage of them both dancing and bopping about at home to the song, which really captured the incredible spirit, fun, and love for life that Granny Nancy possessed. At that time, Granny was 106 and the oldest independently-living woman in Ireland. It was a privilege and an honour to know and have met the inimitable Nancy Stewart.

CIARAN MULLOOLY - *Former RTE Midlands Correspondent*

Nancy Stewart - a Lady For All The Ages

Nancy Stewart was born on 16 October 1913 and had experienced both the Spanish Flu [1918-1920] and the coronavirus pandemic when I met her at her home on the Meath/Westmeath border some years back. It was the occasion of 107th birthday and Nancy's family had gathered in great numbers and in great spirits to celebrate her birthday and hear her great message of hope, which she recorded with the assistance of her granddaughter Louise.

"Imagine turning 107 in a world pandemic," Nancy said to me that day, "this definitely is something very unusual, even for me and all I have been through. I live in Clonard in County Meath and have lived in my home for over eighty three years. I write to you today to send you my love and to offer you my prayers. We are in a very difficult time at the moment in our country, in our lives and in our world. But I reach out to you in this letter to offer you hope, faith and belief that everything will be ok in the end."

A year earlier I had been in the same house just off the old Kinnegad to Enfield road at Clonard. On that memorable day Nancy had been in equally buoyant mood in the midst of her family as the 106-year-old called on the government of the day to get the finger out and provide proper homes for the homeless, as well as the poor and needy in society. The great thing about meeting Nancy was that she was always so seriously conscientious with her message. At the 106th birthday we chatted about so many things that had happened in Irish history down through all her days yet here she was in a frail but healthy state and still saving her pension money to try to support those suffering from poverty in Ireland and abroad.

I recorded an interview with her that day for RTE Television and radio and it got one of the largest responses I ever received over a career lasting well beyond twenty five years in broadcasting. Looking into the camera, with a wicked sense of urgency in her voice, Nancy said the Minister for Housing needed to provide homes at an affordable rate for the many people around the country who have no home of their own and were staying in hotels and other accommodation. Hale and hearty at the age of 106, Nancy talked with great gusto about the true feeling of safety and security that only comes to any family with the peace and comfort of knowing there's a roof over your head for you and your family at the end of every day - especially in the Irish winter. She sat there doing the interview in the house where she had lived for more than 80 years as if to emphasise this point and spoke with great determination and enthusiasm about her mission - making very little of the fact that day that she herself had just broken her hip the previous December yet she had since made a full recovery at one hundred and six years of age and was able to stand up and blow out the candles at the celebration.

Nancy always spoke candidly when we did our interviews She once said to me that the secret to her long life and success has been her abstinence from alcohol and cigarettes, but principally her good humour.

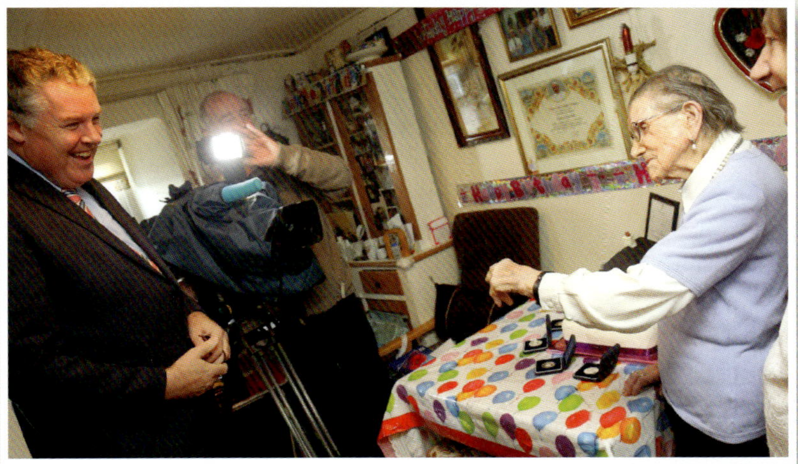

"Not fighting with anybody is good for your health," she told me, adding that she has little time for telephones and gadgets and walked and cycled most of her life. Nancy also spoke with great clarity about the arrival of the 'black and tans' at her home when she was a young child. She described to me how her mother had sent herself and her siblings well down into the garden at the back of the house for safety and shelter when the 'black and tans' came into sight. They had all hidden there and watched with a sense of great fear and anxiety as the man from the unit came through the garden gate and asked for a drink in the home. A few moments later, he was given a jug of milk and bade her farewell but you could tell it had been an uneasy few minutes for the children, locked away down the garden, as they waited to see their own mother's fate at the hands of these notoriously violent visitors.

Nancy had no great wealth or riches - no palace, no staff and certainly no grandeur about her - like many of the other great ladies of the last one hundred years. She said she suffered like everybody else from corporal punishment at school, but the parents of a fellow school pupil had put that to an end by threatening the teacher who was doing it. There was a sense of great pride and courage in her voice as she recalled how they dealt with that challenge from a bully - and survived the ordeal by reacting in the only way one can do when dealing with a bully and that's to confront that person - head on.

Nancy lived with her husband and her family at their modest little home in Clonard for over eighty years. Up to a very short time before her death she still lived in the house with her granddaughter Louise Coghlan, who always described her as the greatest Granny in the world.

Louise adored her Granny and, in fact, I often slagged her that she had become Nancy's media agent - welcoming the TV and radio stations of the world into the house alongside the print and electronic media for endless interviews and chats - and the best part of all that was the fact that Nancy clearly enjoyed every moment of it.

Right until the very end, Nancy held onto her great dignity and her pride. She was a wonderful lady - a great person and a tremendous mother and grandmother. It was a great personal pleasure to meet her. She will be fondly missed.

MIKE MCBRIDE - ***BBC Northern Ireland Journalist***

As a journalist some stories stick with you. Some are incredibly harrowing stories that are difficult to shake, but other stories make you stop and simply smile every time you think back on them.

I was incredibly fortunate during the height of the Covid-19 pandemic to come across Granny Nancy and her granddaughter, Louise. I was scrolling through social media one day when I came across a Facebook post from Louise Coghlan, which simply said that her one hundred and seven year old grandmother from Clonard, County Meath, was attempting a virtual Mass tour across Ireland while in lockdown from the comfort of her very own kitchen. My eyes lit up. I actually had to re-read the post again because I couldn't quite believe what I had read at first.

During the course of the Covid-19 pandemic to come across any positive story, when news was so relentlessly morbid, was quite rare but to come across a story as lovely and as pure as this one was truly remarkable. I instantly tried to make contact with Louise and Granny Nancy, as she was affectionately known, hoping that they would be willing to be interviewed. I managed to organise a Zoom interview with Louise and Nancy, who had both been cooped up together in a house for the whole of lockdown. What struck me most when speaking with them was just how incredibly happy and positive they both were. I don't think I've ever actually met two people with such an incredibly optimistic outlook on life. When many people were understandably fed up of lockdown and constant restrictions being imposed, here was two people who had every right to be annoyed in their current predicament that simply got on with it and made the most of their situation.

Granny Nancy and Louise were both incredibly chatty and many times when I was speaking with them I felt like I was the one being interviewed. They were incredibly warm, friendly and funny - Granny Nancy had a particularly wicked sense of humour and an incredibly infectious laugh. Their story was shared to the BBC News Northern Ireland page on 10 January 2020, and within minutes took off. It was shared to the main BBC News website, radio stations and TV news channels were soon interested and before long more and more news agencies from around the globe were trying to cover the story. Granny Nancy's story was read hundreds of thousands of times and was being read all over the world from Belfast to Bangladesh. What was incredibly poignant was to read the comments underneath the story. People were praising just how wonderful this incredible woman was and saying how delighted they were to read something positive at a time when there wasn't many things to be happy about.

One comment read: 'What a heart-warming story to wake up and read. So pure and beautiful'. It was a pleasure to play a very small part in sharing Granny Nancy's incredibly story to a wider audience.

MAIREAD RONAN ***-TV Presenter and Broadcaster***

During a time when we were all struggling - October 2020 I was so lucky to get to talk to the legend Nancy Stewart on her 107th birthday live on Today FM. Of all the interviews I've done on radio over the years, my chat with Nancy has stayed with me to this day. Her positivity, kindness and message of hope genuinely touched so many of the listeners too.

At the time, many people were feeling anxious and stressed and couldn't see when all this Covid stuff would end. But there I was conversing with Nancy, an exceptional human being who had lived through two world wars, the other pandemic, multiple recessions and got through it all with a sense of humour and was still so obviously full of love. Nancy's secret which she was kind enough to share with my audience was simple but solid - "Eat plenty of good food and be kind to your neighbour, try not to be too angry with anyone". Excellent advice and when I've felt myself get unreasonably cranky I think of Nancy's words. She also confirmed something that lockdown had taught us and that is the importance of our family, friends, neighbours and . . . of course cake!

Louise her wonderful granddaughter, told me that Granny had a great saying each day before opening the curtains "Open them up and let God's light in". I loved the phrase so much, and I hope Nancy won't mind but I've used it in my own home ever since meeting her on air. Now my five year old Eliza says it every day too, "Mum, we have to let God's light in".

Thanks Nancy for giving me so much hope in what was a really difficult time, and to Louise for sharing your lovely Granny Nancy with all of us . X

WALLIS BIRD - ***Irish Award Winning Musician***
Nancy and Lou, what a team. Their craic and connection was something special that moved past the now into the beyond. Because it moved people. Two good eggs nested together, forever and always.

SAHM VENTER - ***Journalist and Editor of 'The Prison Letters of Nelson Mandela'***
An enthusiastic voice on the end of a WhatsApp call, Louise Coghlan, led me through the remarkable Covid-19 lockdown existence she had fashioned for her beloved Granny Nancy.

Living in a little bubble in a quaint Irish country home, they centred their life together around endless cups of tea, rich imaginings, a hilarious sense of humour, and a laptop.

Louise's idea to bring online mass to her grandmother, Nancy Stewart, was genius. Not only did it help lift the spirits of the one hundred and seven year old who was missing church, but it drew the two of them even closer.

What set Granny Nancy apart was not so much her concern about having to stay indoors, but rather how everyone else was coping. After all, she had already lived through another pandemic, two world wars, and her own set of personal tragedies.

Louise introduced Granny Nancy to the idea of communicating through WIFI, air pods, headphones, and creating live videos for whoever wanted to watch them. Facebook helped her build a cross-continental family for which she would become the adopted matriarch, urging them to follow the rules and to always 'look up'.

It wasn't long before she was giving radio and television interviews from her tiny sitting room, transmitting her infectious joy in defiance of the long, dark winter that surrounded us all..

It struck me on my first meeting with Louise, shortly after Granny Nancy's death, that she was a storyteller bursting with detail about their antics as well as anecdotes about her grandmother's wisdom and nurturing nature.

She has written a book we can all relate to, that generations to come will benefit from. The tale of a grandmother and granddaughter navigating an international emergency and how they invited us all in, to live and love and learn with them.

LOUISE WALSH - ***Journalist and LMFM Radio Producer***

I can't even remember how I came to know Nancy Stewart and her partner-in-crime, the ever-smiling Louise but it seems like I knew her forever.

Nancy and Louise were a team. A team made stronger by the boundaries of Covid-19 when they isolated away together, but became more connected with the rest of the world through their hilarious online blogs. Nancy was one hundred and seven years young. Her body aged but her mind, spirit and heart stayed eternally young. She always had that mischievous glint in her eye and would always be up for the chats and the craic and opening her doors to everyone. There were no strangers in Nancy's world, only friends who hadn't yet had a cup of tea with her. In lockdown especially, Nancy's bond with her granddaughter Louise was tangible. The pair were always laughing together and Louise always brought out the best in her. There never seemed to be rain in Clonard, only sun until the clouds appeared to mourn Nancy's passing.

We only saw glimpses into their Covid-19 Clonard world but we had no doubt, we wanted to see more. To feel involved more and to laugh more. We wanted to say we were friends with Nancy and Louise.

That world will now come to light through Louise's book about the times she shared with her adored gran. Nancy was Louise's world and Louise was Nancy's world. And we can now be a little of that world.

Nancy Stewart will never be too far away once Louise continues to smile and make people happy. It was a privilege and honour to be allowed to write some articles with them both and I will always treasure those encounters.

18 COMEDIAN'S HOME TRUTHS
HAS TOMMY LOST HIS NAVAN ROOTS?

15 THE GAVAN REILLY COLUMN
ARE WE ALL IN THIS TOGETHER?

IN PRINT | ONLINE | ON THE GO

Meath Chronicle

Saturday 17 October, 2020 — www.meathchronicle.ie €2.90 (£2)

'Look up and smile even if you have your mask on'

LOUISE WALSH

WISDOM Inspirational great grandmother Nancy Stewart pens heart-warming letter of hope ahead of her 107th birthday

ONE of Ireland's oldest residents has written a public letter of hope, ahead of her 107th birthday, urging people to take care of each other during the current pandemic.

Nancy Stewart has survived two World Wars, the War of Independence and the 1918 flu pandemic and has been cocooning since March at her home in Clonard where she has lived for the last 83 years.

She admits that she is feeling isolated from the regular crowds that usually visit her home and is too afraid to venture out because of Covid-19.

Visitors to her home are now severely restricted to carers, medics and some family members, all of whom have to sanitize stringently and wear masks at all times.

Nancy turns 107 this Friday, 16th October and continues to astound her family with her resilience and positivity.

She has just recovered from a chronic chest infection, from which loved ones feared she would not recover.

Now in a heart-warming open letter Nancy has sent her love and prayers to all with the firm belief that there is light at the end of this Covid-19 tunnel.

"We are in a very difficult time at the moment in our country, in our lives and in our world. But I reach out to you in this letter to offer you hope, faith and belief that everything will be ok in the end.

"We are in another stage of this battle against the virus but we will get through this. Like everything I've been through since the day I was born in 1913, no matter how bad things have got, I'm the living proof that we can survive and in years to come, this will just be a distant memory.

"We must mind ourselves but we must also mind all those around us. Look up and smile even if you have your mask on.

"We are not here to live for ourselves but to live for each other."

» READ NANCY'S FULL LETTER ON PAGE 62

'We must mind ourselves but we must also mind all those around us' says Nancy Stewart who will turn 107 this week.

Higher visibility policing to be a priority for new Navan Garda Superintendent - P17

A special thanks to Gavan Becton, Editor of The Meath Chronicle for sharing this with us for the book.

NEWS

'A heroic and gentle lady, a true neighbour and a steadfast friend'

LEGEND Clonard says goodbye to much loved Nancy Stewart who passed away peacefully last Friday at the age of 107

ANN CASEY

CLONARD'S Nancy Stewart who died peacefully on Friday just a month short of her 108th birthday was described as "an inspiration to millions of people" and "a living saint," at her funeral mass on Sunday at in St Finian's Church, Clonard.

Beloved... Nancy Stewart.

Believed to have been the oldest woman in Ireland, she was also described as "a heroic and gentle lady, a loving mother, grandmother, great grandmother and great-great grandmother, a true neighbour and a steadfast friend."

Chief concelebrant, Fr John Keegan said she was always ready to give a helping hand to a neighbour in need.

"She was always willing to go the extra mile with the one who needed support.

"Her generous heart extended beyond the confines of the parish. She helped near and far and in particular people in distant lands though her generous donations and support."

Fr Breen told the congregation she had died in her own home at Towlagh, Clonard, in her own bed with her much loved daughter Olive and granddaughter Louise by her side.

Fr Breen said he had been in awe of her and considered her a living saint.

"I first met her when she was a sprightly 101 years old. She told me how her husband died in 1989 and she had been seriously injured herself.

"That accident happened as they were turning into this church to go to Mass.

"And yet with the unquestioning faith of a saint, Nancy said she accepted God's will.

"She also said that whenever we are faced with tragedies we must trust God and believe he will make all things right in the end.

"From that moment on, I was in awe of Nancy and considered her a living saint."

Nancy received birthday cards from all over the country.

Fr Breen said it was no exaggeration to say that because of the way her granddaughter Louise had creatively used the Facebook social media platform, "many millions of people worldwide had been inspired by Nancy's wise words, simple faith and sincere prayer, since the beginning of the pandemic.

"A light has gone out in the hearts of her family, the local community and millions of people worldwide.

"A really great person has departed this world."

Fr Tom Gilroy and Fr Declan Murray also participated in the ceremony and burial in St Finian's cemetery.

Anne (Nancy) Stewart, nee Bird was born in October 2013 in Castlerickard.

She was predeceased by her husband, Bob, her twin daughters Margaret and Ann and sons in law Joe and Michael.

She is survived by her children, Finian (Bob), Kathleen, Mary and Olive, her daughter in law Alcoque, sons in law Des, John, Mattie, grandchildren, great-grandchildren, great-great-grandchildren, nieces and nephews, her much-loved carers, neighbours and her many friends.

In a poignant post on social media, granddaughter Louise Coghlan wrote: "What will I do without my beautiful smiling Nancy? Broken heart waking up this morning to only one cup of tea needing to be made...this incoming grief is going to be a titanic heartbreak in my life but one thing I'm sure, Nancy definitley put on my life jacket before she left, I just need to float."

> " You also should look on the bright side all the time, no matter what. Don't dwell on the past -
> **Nancy Stewart**

Local councillor, Joe Fox who presented Nancy with a certificate and flowers on her 107th birthday said she was "an inspirational woman with a brilliant attitude to life."

Cllr Joe Fox meeting Nancy on her 107th birthday.

In the early days of the coronavirus Nancy appealed to people not to panic buy or stress and then last October at the age of 107, she penned an open letter to the people of Ireland which caught the imagination of the nation.

"We are in another stage of this battle against the virus but we will get through this. Like everything I've been through since the day I was born in 1913, no matter how bad things have got, I'm the living proof that we can survive and in years to come, this will just be a distant memory."

Louise Coghlan, granddaughter of Nancy, helps display her haul of President's Medals on the occasion of her 106th birthday.

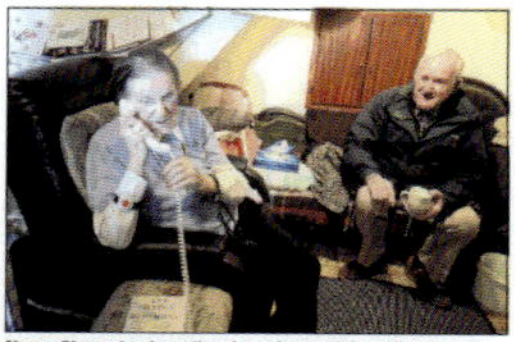

Nancy Stewart gets on the phone to speak to wellwishers as neighbour Paddy Dolan looks on with a cup of tea.
PHOTOS: SEAMUS FARRELLY

When Nancy celebrated her 107th birthday last year, her beloved Clonard community was determined to mark the occasion in style.

Cars arrived in their hundreds at Clonard GAA grounds with balloons, bunting and special 'Nancy 107' number plates as the wellwishers prepared to set off in convoy to Nancy's cottage a mile from the village.

Nancy, however, had other ideas and arrived at the grounds in her granddaughter and carer Louise's Coghlan's car. She smiled out from the window while enthusiastically waving the Tricolour, thanking the startled volunteers she'd caught by surprise.

Nancy attributed her long life to "good food, good friends and staying positive."

"You also should look on the bright side all the time, no matter what. Don't dwell on the past," she said.

GRANNY NANCY'S BIRTHDAY'S FROM 100 TO 107 YEARS YOUNG!

Photos by Elaine McCrossan

Photos by Elaine McCrossan

Photos by Elaine McCrossan

Myself and Gran on her 106th birthday.
Thank you Seamus Farrelly for this photo!

This photo was taken by Elaine McCrossan

I took this photo and I just think the seven medals along with the cake epitomise the fun and magic of Granny. Every year from 100 years old, Granny received a medal from the President of Ireland. Granny was very proud of these medals.

This painting was created by Granny Nancy's grandson Colm Maye who is a wonderfully gifted Irish artist. To view more of Colm's work, do pop along to: https://www.instagram.com/colmmaye

CHAPTER FIFTEEN
ACKNOWLEDGMENTS

Those who have helped spread the good news of Granny Nancy:

Elaine McCrossan - Elaine was so kind to help me locate photos from Granny's birthday's. I was so grateful to you for helping me out with these and for taking such gorgeous photos of Gran over the years.

Seamus Farrelly - Thank you for sending me on photos of Gran that you took at her 106th birthday.

Gavan Becton - Thanks so much for all your support during the years and a special mention for your support with Gran's 107th birthday. We will never forget that magic.

Pat McLoughlin - for your lifetime of friendship and for all the beautiful words you wrote about Nancy over the years. She loved you Pat and she never held back from telling you! So many cups of tea and laughs.

The Topic Newspapers, Midlands 103, KFM, LMFM, Today Fm, RTE, Ireland AM and all media outlets across the country and across the world - A big thank you to all who have supported the spreading of the good news of Granny Nancy down through the many years and particularly a special mention to so many people who have supported me with the release of this book.

A special mention to all the carers who helped mind Granny over her lifetime. You all played a very special part in Granny living such a wonderful life in her own home and she loved you all dearly. You were vital to her long life and most importantly her happiness. Also a special mention here to Dr. Katie Lee of Kinnegad who without her help, Granny would not have lived her last years at home. Thank you Dr. Katie, I will never forget what you did for Granny but for me also. You are an exceptional doctor with a very special heart!

Gran's family - Kathleen and Des, Finian and Alacoque, Mary and John, Olive and Joe [RIP], Mattie and Anne [RIP] and Margaret [RIP] and Michael [RIP] - remembering all of Gran's closest as they have known and loved her the longest and she loved them all dearly. All of Gran's grandchildren, great grandchildren and great great grandchildren who were another injection of love for Granny. Of course all the Bird and Harnan family and all extended family who Granny was so proud of and loved dearly. So many people loved and cared for Gran and a lifetime of friendship was shared!

Gran's friends and neighbours - Too many to mention here but a special mention to Mary and Tony Maher who have been Gran's immediate neighbours for all her life and never failed to love and care for her in so many ways also. Gran loved all her neighbours on the road and in the community of Clonard. She was a very proud Clonard woman and her friends were as important to her as her family. Gran loved the community of Clonard and was involved in the Altar Society and the Active Retirement group for a lifetime and a half. The Active Retirement group were her dearest of friends and I know she would love for me to give them a special mention here.

Granny pictured with all her wonderful friends of Clonard Active Retirement Group. Thanks to Breda Twomey for contributing this photo.

A final word to Gran's many friends across the county, country and world. Anyone that was a friend of Nancy's knew how much they were loved as she would smile from ear to ear when they visited, called or communicated by letters or card so I hope you know, if you were a friend of Nancy's, you are remembered here too.

Gran loved baking apple tarts and we both loved eating them with a big cup of tea or five. She also was famous for sharing them among her friends, family and neighbours over the years.

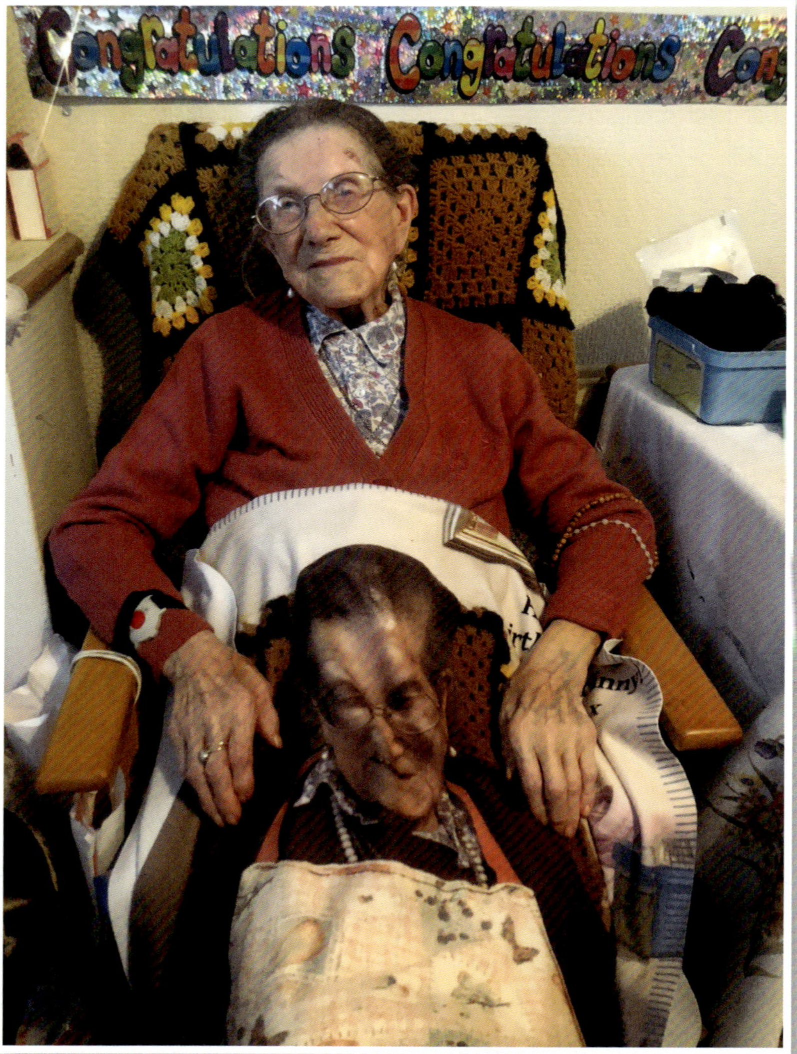

Gran got so much fun out of the blanket I bought her for her 107th birthday. Gran would say "Well Nancy how are you today? It's younger you are getting?" as she picked up the blanket. It was all about the laughter with the two of us and Gran was the best for instigating it.

CHAPTER SIXTEEN

THANK YOU

Where do I start and where do I end when it comes to the thank you section of this story.

In my life I have been blessed with so many good people around me. From friends to family to more friends, my life has been a gift in the area of having good people close to me and as I like to call them, my inner circle. Good people who see me for me and who not only allow me to be me, but also encourage and support any ideas I come up with.

This section is for **YOU** reading this. First and foremost, you have bought this book and you have no idea how much that means to me and I want to remind you, that **I see you and thank you from the bottom of my heart**.

My special words of thanks must go to the following people:

Mam who is my rock and guiding light. I would not have being able to do any of this or maybe even been able to cope with the emptiness within me if not for having mam by my side. A big thanks to my sister **Claire** and my brother **Justin** who are always there for me and of course **Anthony [Snr.], Anthony, Nathan, Lauren, Josh** and **Shauna** and my **Aunt Ro** too. You all have being a wonderful support to me over my life and I could not have done this without you. A special mention to the lady of the hour and the reason this book is even a book - the amazing **Granny Nancy**. She fought the good fight, she ran the race and she kept the faith. She was my best friend and I will never forget you Gran and I will never stop loving you. Until we meet in Heaven until that times comes, I will keep looking up to you x

My family, Kathleen and Des, Mary and John, Finian and Alacoque, Mattie, my cousins and all my extended family for their support and of course the wonderful Bird and Harnan Family!

My best friends **Denise Martin** [for all those phonecalls and for being you], **Martha Dalton** [for everything you have helped me with in life, for helping make this book happen, I couldn't have done this without you], **Lorraine and Claire Mullally** [for all the chats and a lifetime of friendship since we were five years old], **Catriona Nurney** [for the seven million coffees and chats], **Rosaleen Cusack** [for just always being there and helping with all my mad ideas over my life], **Denise Cusack** [for being you], **Paddy and Dinah Maguire** [for being such good friends to our family and how we will never forget their kindness], **Ursula Heeney** [for your beautiful heart and for being a wonderful friend always]. I also would like to mention my loyal and lovely Edenderry circle of friends - **Yvonne Mahon, Sinead Mullally, Emer Goode Gallagher, Mandy Kelly, Emma Hampton, Siobhan O'Neill and Michelle Poland** [for all those coffees, laughs and chats] and so many more people who I love dearly. I hope you know even if you do not see your name here, how much you mean to me and all you have contributed in so many ways over the years to me writing this book. This book was not written over the last twelve months so to speak but more over a lifetime of writing, living, learning, losing and my favourite part - LOVING so many of ye all and ye returning so much love to me.

My writing community in **London Writers Salon** - A special shout out to some dear friends of mine who have been in my writing boat with me since the start of this process on January 5th. A special mention to those who have put on my lifejacket a number of times through this deeply moving, lonely and loving writing experience. A special mention to **Lauren Deborah** who during a 24 writing sprint literally saved me from the sea of grief and helped me to handle my broken heart with such compassion that she allowed and helped me complete the first draft of this book. I will be forever grateful to you Lauren for that moment and for your wonderful friendship ever since. I can guarantee you this book would not have happened without that moment Lauren and for you giving of yourself to help me.

Thank you to **Tracy O'Brien** for endless good morning messages, smiles and support galore, **Linda Sach [and Ruby] and Marian Edmunds** for so many conversations and a lifetime of friendship ahead of us, **Iesha Denize** for seeing something in me, saying it to me and supporting me, **Mark from Boston** for all our weekly check in's and for your belief in me I will be forever grateful.

Thank you to **Kathryn Koromilas, Lindsey Trout Hughes, Lauren McMenemy, Kimberlee Walker, Shalini Nina, Viv Speers, Regina Beach, Molly Ovenden, Debbie Kraus, Sue Ransom, Beth Collier** and so many of the LWS team/hosts who I just adore and am so grateful to have in my life. To **Melissa Weidmann** who is just a magic poet with such a gorgeous heart, **Siddhi [Sid] Upadhyaya** from Ohio for all those fun cabin times, **Leone Gabrielle, Sarah and Michelle Mansfield** for so many late night chats and laughs and so many more who have helped and healed me. A special shout out to the **Weekend Writers** family also.

I am a writer and I am a very proud supporter of my writing friends and would love if you might follow their links to their works and support them anyway you can. I know I wouldn't have written this book without them by my side. This is only a tiny portion of the many talented and wonderful people who I now count as friends.

There are so many I could list, I could fill this book with all the talent I've met over the last twelve months but here are just a few of my closest friends, gifted writers they all are and very magic humans! I'm so lucky to have found ye all.

Lauren Deborah - Canada and Australia
https://laurendeborah.substack.com

Tracy O'Brien - Isle of Wight
https://tracyobrien.substack.com

Marian Edmunds - Australia
https://theparadigmshuffle.substack.com

Iesha Denize - London
https://www.instagram.com/iesha.denize

Kathryn Kormilas - Scotland
kathrynkoromilas.com/

Mark Censky - Boston
https://medium.com/@markjosephcensky

Julie Russell - Nottinghamshire, UK
www.instagram.com/the_bread_witch

Melissa Weidmann - Cape Codd
https://spontaneopoet.com

Lindsey Trout Hughes - New York
www.lindseytrouthughes.com

Shalini Nina
https://shallbe.medium.com

Jenny Hammerton
https://www.silverscreensuppers.com

Paul Sockett
www.paulsockett.com

Nessa Chileshe
www.instagram.com/nessa.chileshe

Sue Du Feu - France
https://lettersfromajerseymother.blogspot.com

Emma Rhind Tutt
https://www.instagram.com/rabbitholeamnesia/

Emily Reid - Costa Rica
https://writersrising.org

Jo Blackshaw - Wales
jojourneys.net

Lauren McMenemy - London
laurenmc.carrd.co

Regina Beach - Wales
www.reginagbeach.com

Molly Ovenden - Minnesota
www.mollyovenden.com

Sofia Koutlaki - London
www.sofiakoutlaki.com/

Ant Heald - Wales
inertiapreneur.com

Nicolas Laborie - London
www.nicolaslaborie.com

Patricia Lane - Massachusetts
instagram.com/planewrite

Susannah Rigg - Mexico
www.susannahrigg.com

Madeline Wahl - Florida/Scotland
www.madelinehwahl.com

Twinkle Burke - New York
https://www.linkedin.com/in/twinkle-burke-7884766/

Jodi Hausen - Montana
www.jodihausen.com

Sasha Soreff - New York
https://sashasoreffdance.com

William Wonders
www.qfproduction.com/

Jane Cahane - UK
https://smallwriteratlarge.com

Erica Sharlette
https://www.linkedin.com/in/ericasharlettewriter/

Simone Talfourd
https://www.instagram.com/misstalfourd/

Linda Sach
https://www.instagram.com/ljs_stille/

Elaine Kasket
www.elainekasket.com

London Writer's Salon
www.londonswriterssalon.com

London Writers Salon - A special thank you to **Matt, Parul** and all my LWS Family. This book would not have happened without you! I will never forget the endless supply of love, support and kindness you have shown me over the last year and I will be forever on your team or anything you need help with! Thank you from the bottom of my heart! We're friends for life now and my apartment light will always be on for each of ye and know you will forever have a friend in little old Ireland who loves you dearly and believes in your writing! Writing Hours, Cabin times, Marathons and Sprints [and I don't even like running], Socials, Goal setting workshops, interviews - we've done it all together and I owe you so much.

A special mention to **Fr. John Keegan** and **Fr. Gerard Breen**. Fr. John Keegan who has been a friend of Granny for all her life and who was so good to her in so many ways over the years and also gave Granny the very special send off to Heaven that I know she would have loved. A very special thanks to Fr. Gerard Breen, who carried us through the loss of my dad eight years ago and a person who Granny absolutely adored. Thank you Fr. Breen for your wonderful foreword which means so much to me.

I'd like to thank all who contributed to this book. I was blown away by your words, time, effort and absolute kindness. I asked and you came back tenfold and I'll never be able to thank you all enough for your support of Granny's story and for helping me tell it in this very special way. A word of thanks to **Ciaran Mullooly Eddie Rowley, Mairead Ronan, Sahm Venter, Louise Ferriter, Fr. Richard Gibbon, Anne Marie Kelly, Wallis Bird, Luan Parle, Mike McBride, Cliona O'Hagan and Fr. Bryan Shortall**. I am honoured to call you all my friends!

This final space is very much a thank you which I kept for last. The final thank you must go to my wonderful **'Living and Laughing with Lou'**

Facebook Family. I have no words for each and every one of you. You entered my life at a time I decided I'd just chance my arm and set up a page to have a bit of fun and you have stayed with me from that day to this. The fact that you have stayed means more to me than you will ever know. I love you dearly and I don't know what I would have done without you in so many ways. I cannot wait to meet you in real life and even if we never get to meet, it actually doesn't matter because we will be friends for life. Granny was our connection and that will never leave us and I will always be so grateful to the way you embraced our messing and now you support me in ways I will never be able to express. From our baking to our prayers, to our singing to my ranting, to joke telling, to dressing up, to smiling and laughing, to crying and consoling, to hoping and having, to losing and leaving, to Facebook lives that were unforgettable to the days where we just sat with each other, to the moments where we had no words to how we were feeling to the days where you can't shut me up. From the blue skies to the green grass, to the rain falling and the snow surrounding us, to the storms and the skylines, from the sunsets to the moon rising, looking for stars and talking to the sun, we've done it all and yet we have so much more to do. I will be forever grateful for the support you gave me to enjoy and embrace Granny. How you took us under your wings, how you helped me cope on the days I didn't know could I keep going to the day of Gran's 107th birthday and all the days in between, to the day we let Gran go to the days where I've been trying to find my feet and in many ways, find myself. To today where I am so proud of each and every one of you and I bless myself twice to know I have friends for life not only all over the country but all over the world. You mean everything to me and you always will.

Love and light always and don't forget, **KEEP LOOKING UP**!

Your friend forever,
Lou x
PS. I'll let you in a little secret since you have read all this way down - Exciting news . . . I've starting writing my next book. It will be a little different but it's on its way. Watch this space as they say x

Happy Birthday Happy Birthday